Second Edition

ARCHERY
Fundamentals

10

Second Edition

ARCHERY
Fundamentals

Teresa Johnson

Human Kinetics

Library of Congress Cataloging-in-Publication Data

Archery fundamentals / Human Kinetics with Teresa Johnson. -- Second edition.
   pages cm
1. Archery. I. Johnson, Teresa, 1977- II. Human Kinetics (Organization)
GV1185.A74 2014
799.3'2--dc23

                     2014018178

ISBN: 978-1-4504-6910-4 (print)

This book is a revised edition of *Archery Fundamentals* by Douglas Engh, published in 2005 by Human Kinetics.

The web addresses cited in this text were current as of June 2014, unless otherwise noted.

Acquisitions Editor: Tom Heine; **Developmental Editor:** Carla Zych; **Managing Editor:** Rachel Fowler; **Copyeditor:** Patsy Fortney; **Permissions Manager:** Martha Gullo; **Graphic Designer:** Keri Evans; **Graphic Artist:** Tara Welsch; **Cover Designer:** Keith Blomberg; **Photograph (cover):** © Human Kinetics; **Photographs (interior):** Neil Bernstein, unless otherwise noted; photos on pages 4, 9, and 146 © Teresa Johnson; **Photo Asset Manager:** Laura Fitch; **Visual Production Assistant:** Joyce Brumfield; **Photo Production Manager:** Jason Allen; **Art Manager:** Kelly Hendren; **Associate Art Manager:** Alan L. Wilborn; **Illustrations:** © Human Kinetics, unless otherwise noted; **Printer:** United Graphics

Human Kinetics books are available at special discounts for bulk purchase. Special editions or book excerpts can also be created to specification. For details, contact the Special Sales Manager at Human Kinetics.

Printed in the United States of America   10 9 8 7 6 5 4 3 2 1

The paper in this book is certified under a sustainable forestry program.

Human Kinetics
Website: www.HumanKinetics.com

United States: Human Kinetics
P.O. Box 5076
Champaign, IL 61825-5076
800-747-4457
e-mail: humank@hkusa.com

Canada: Human Kinetics
475 Devonshire Road Unit 100
Windsor, ON N8Y 2L5
800-465-7301 (in Canada only)
e-mail: info@hkcanada.com

Europe: Human Kinetics
107 Bradford Road
Stanningley
Leeds LS28 6AT, United Kingdom
+44 (0) 113 255 5665
e-mail: hk@hkeurope.com

Australia: Human Kinetics
57A Price Avenue
Lower Mitcham, South Australia 5062
08 8372 0999
e-mail: info@hkaustralia.com

New Zealand: Human Kinetics
P.O. Box 80
Torrens Park, South Australia 5062
0800 222 062
e-mail: info@hknewzealand.com

E6168

Contents

Introduction

Welcome to the sport of archery! This modern sport with ancient roots has grown in recent years to become one of the world's fastest-growing Olympic sports. Those who participate in the sport are offered a wide range of equipment options and ways to enjoy the sport. Nearly every culture in the world has created some form of archery in its history—for survival, combat, and competition. More recently, archery has been at the forefront of pop culture, making appearances in films such as *The Hunger Games* and *Brave*, and it was one of the most-watched sports at the London 2012 Olympic Games.

The sport of archery has a rich history and a solid place in our culture. In Britain, under the rule of James II, golf was once banned because it interfered with archery tournaments used to train archers for national defense. Archery tournaments and festivals remained strong in Europe long after bows were replaced by gunpowder for defense. Archery evolved into a competitive sport not only in Europe but also in Asia and the United States. Following the U.S. Civil War, two Confederate veterans, Will and Maurice Thompson, learned to hunt and shoot with bows and arrows. Maurice's widely read book, *Witchery of Archery*, highlighted their exploits with archery and served to stimulate national interest in the sport. Archery became an official Olympic sport in 1900, and a flaming arrow was used to light the Olympic flame during the opening ceremonies of the Barcelona Summer Olympics in 1992. The National Aeronautics and Space Administration (NASA) has sent ceremonial arrows into outer space. More recently, fashion designers have begun using archery in their runway shows and in store window displays; countless video games and apps feature archery; and film stars, musicians, and athletes from other sports are now frequently seen with bows in hand.

Target archery has evolved into a variety of sports and challenges for both youth and adults. In the Olympic Games, and at competitions sanctioned by USA Archery—the national governing body for the sport in the United States—archers shoot targets at a fixed distance that is determined by their age and equipment style. Field and 3D archery also offer archers their choice of fun, challenging games to try. Each type of archery offers a different kind of excitement. There are also numerous choices for equipment, including the "trad bow," a wooden recurve or longbow, which speaks to a traditional, minimalist approach; the Olympic-style recurve bow with elongated limbs, aiming aids, and stabilization options; and the compound bow, which is a more compact bow aided by cams and wheels.

Whichever option you choose, know that you have the flexibility to move among equipment styles, and that each type of equipment can help you to be more successful with other bow options. Whether you want to enjoy archery recreationally or competitively, there is a discipline for you and an organization to help you participate, find a coach, compete, and take your shooting to the next level if you so choose. These organizations sanction clubs, host tournaments, create rules for scoring, and develop proven training methods for both archers and their coaches. This book will guide you through the fundamentals of archery so that you can quickly become proficient in this exciting sport.

Many communities have archery ranges or clubs where the sport can be enjoyed. As you learn the sport, you can seek out a club for a safe place to shoot. The sport of archery is inherently safe, and recent studies, even by the U.S. National Institutes of Health, show that archery has one of the lowest rates of injury of all outdoor sports (www.ncbi.nlm.nih.gov/pubmed/22648468). Be sure to visit your local archery range or pro shop to find out where you can enjoy the sport in your area; the staff can help you get started on the path to becoming an archer!

Outdoor Target Range Design

Archery has a very good safety record because of the constant attention to safety in planning archery shooting ranges. Ranges can be set up outdoors or indoors with a variety of configurations according to the discipline. Field archery, for example, requires a roving course, which is often constructed in a wooded area. The sport of 3D archery—in which people shoot at foam animal targets at either known or unknown distances—employs a similar range setup. Target archery is literally a bit more straightforward and requires a flat, open area that is anywhere from 15 to 90 yards long, depending on the type of competition. Some ranges are small enough to fit in a schoolyard or residential backyard, and some are so huge that they take up many acres and are managed by clubs or recreation departments.

The basic outdoor target range looks like a large box (figure 1). The range should be aligned (if possible) so you are always shooting away from the sun. Access to the range should be blocked except to

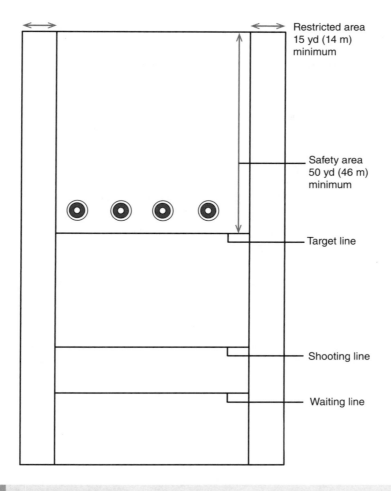

Restricted area
15 yd (14 m)
minimum

Safety area
50 yd (46 m)
minimum

Target line

Shooting line

Waiting line

1   **An archery range.**

guide spectators and newly arriving archers to a designated waiting area behind the line from which archers shoot. Safety ropes, warning signs, and fencing all help, but due diligence is required on the part of archers and range officials to be on the lookout for people suddenly appearing where they don't belong.

The range should be free of obstructions and include a safety buffer behind the targets of at least 50 yards. Another option is to have the archery range back up to a hillside or berm. Archery ranges should be free of rocks, tree limbs, branches, and the like, and grass should be kept mowed to facilitate locating lost arrows or other dropped items. Although there is no specific size requirement for a target archery range, safety guidelines include having at least 50 yards behind the target if no natural backstop or barrier is present to stop errant arrows, and at least 15 yards of clear and restricted space on either side of the target. The term *restricted space* refers to the aforementioned taped or roped-off space that clearly tells spectators that an archery event is in progress.

An outdoor target archery range features lined-up target stands that support foam targets. Lines on the field designate where you should stand to shoot at your assigned target. Lines can be painted on the ground using the same equipment used to line soccer and baseball fields; other options are also available. Be sure to check with your local recreation department or town hall about permissible ways to line a field in your locale. Rope or cord is an acceptable alternative if laid flat, but in general, trip hazards are frowned on. If rope or cord is used, it should not be secured.

The *waiting line* is a line behind which you stand when you are waiting your turn to shoot. The *shooting line* is the line you straddle while shooting, and the *target line* is a line in front of the target that acts as a "speed bump" (or temporary stopping place) for archers who are retrieving their arrows. When retrieving your arrows, stop at the target line and wait your turn. This line also prevents excited archers from rushing to the target to see their arrows and potentially hitting the nock ends (outer ends) of the arrows that are sticking out of the target. The target line should be back far enough that arrows sticking out from the target do not cross it.

Safety netting, or backstop netting, specifically made for archery is sometimes suspended behind the targets. Arrows hit the net and drop to the ground in front of it, or become caught in the net. Such netting should *never* be used with the intention of protecting people, animals, or property, but should instead be thought of as a speed bump for the arrows themselves. Arrows from bows of a heavier draw weight (i.e., more powerful bows) often tear through a net without warning. Even arrows from the most lightweight bows occasionally penetrate a net. Therefore, even if a safety net is in position, a designated area behind it should be set up where any arrows that pass through the net can fall safely to the ground.

A *bow rack* is sometimes set up near the waiting line to provide safe storage for bows when they are not being shot. *Ground quivers* are sometimes provided at public ranges to hold arrows upright when not in use; they are often on or directly behind the shooting line, which you straddle while shooting your bow. Ground quivers can be made from traffic cones, plastic plumbers' pipe, or even bent wire. Many archers use portable quivers, which can be attached to the archer by means of a belt. If ground quivers are used, special safety techniques should be used while carrying arrows (see chapter 3).

Indoor Target Range Design

An indoor target archery range is basically an outdoor range in miniature form. An indoor range can be created in a basketball or multisport arena, or at an archery shop. It has the same series of waiting, shooting, and target lines drawn out on the floor using tape or paint stripes. Often, a safety net is used to slow arrows down if they miss the target. Remember, such a net should never be used to protect life or property; it is used simply to catch arrows and allow them to drop to the floor. In general, the more powerful the bow is, the less likely the backstop net will be used to catch the arrow. To safely install backstop netting, be sure to follow the directions provided in the packaging. In general, netting is hung using poles or other hooks, at least 1 yard from any wall.

As with the outdoor target range, the indoor range requires controlled access for spectators. Doors downrange (meaning near the targets) should be closed or blocked, and warning signs that archery is taking place should be posted. Spectators must not be allowed near the shooting line; they should be in a designated spectator area located well behind the waiting line. Be on the lookout for sudden appearances of people where they don't belong, and be ready to stop shooting at any time if a hazard is brought to your attention.

Field or 3D Archery Range Design

An archery range can also be designed to look a little like a small golf course. At a field or 3D archery range, you walk from one shooting position to another in a wooded setting or an open field to shoot at targets laid out in a pattern. You can shoot at standard targets or even at molded foam targets shaped like animals (figure 2). Although the range is set up as a hybrid between a hike and an archery tournament, standard range design rules still apply—access is tightly controlled using fencing, safety barriers, and warning signs, and the targets are positioned so that no archers are ever shooting in the direction of others. Many people who enjoy field or 3D archery comment that these disciplines give them the opportunity to enjoy nature and the sport of archery at the same time—an experience not to be missed.

2   A 3D archery range with foam targets shaped like animals.

Range Safety Rules

Every range should have a person designated as a safety officer. This person can be the supervisor at a pro shop or club, the coach or instructor at a Junior Olympic Archery Development (JOAD) club, or a volunteer at an outdoor archery range. At a tournament, this person will likely be a certified judge, also called a tournament official. It is this person's sole duty to control the archery range in terms of safety and to issue the standard commands to come to the shooting line, shoot, retrieve arrows, and stop shooting. Archers can then concentrate on their shooting and simply listening for the appropriate archery range safety commands or whistles. If you shoot alone, however, it is your responsibility to act as both archer and safety officer. Even though you may not be blowing the standard whistle commands, always keep these commands in mind so that when you do join a group you will be a safe addition to that archery community.

Commit the following list of universally accepted whistle commands to memory, and follow them always. The use of whistles, versus verbal commands, is recommended because it leaves little room for speculation regarding the command. At first, this list might seem out of order, but the single whistle blast is used to signal shooting because many tournaments are timed and the single blast starts the clock. If a range is managed safely, the last whistle command, which signals an emergency, is rarely needed.

- *Two whistle blasts:* Walk from the waiting line to the shooting line, and place one foot on either side of the shooting line, also known as straddling the shooting line. Do not touch any arrows at this time.

- *One whistle blast:* Begin shooting at your assigned target, using your personal equipment or the equipment assigned to you. When you have shot all of your arrows, return to the waiting line.

- *Three whistle blasts:* Retrieve your arrows at this time, walking to the target line and waiting your turn to safely pull your arrows. When all archers have retrieved their arrows, they return to the waiting line, walking and carrying their arrows safely.

- *Four or more whistle blasts.* This important command signals an emergency. Essentially, it means "Stop what you are doing—there is an emergency on the range." If you are drawing back your bow, do not release the string, but instead let down the arrow and stand still on the shooting line to await instructions.

Stretching and Warming Up

Archery is a physical activity, and your body must be prepared prior to shooting. Warm-ups, followed by stretching exercises, are helpful in loosening your muscles and joints. Warm up first and then stretch out, using aids such as a flexible stretch band. Consult your certified archery instructor, coach, or physical trainer about the proper stretching routine for your particular body type and needs. Walking and swinging your arms is a great way to warm up your body and get your blood flowing. You can warm up while setting out your targets and carrying your archery equipment to the shooting line. Following are some key stretches that will help get you ready to shoot some arrows.

ARM EXTENSION

Extend your arms straight over your head, and interlock your hands with your palms facing outward. Stretch your arms upward slowly and hold for 5 to 10 seconds (figure 3).

3   **Arm extension stretch.**

SHOULDER EXTENSION

In turn, gently pull each elbow across your chest toward the opposite shoulder. Hold for 10 seconds (figure 4).

4   **Shoulder extension stretch.**

TRICEPS EXTENSION

Hold your arms up, cradling your head on either side. In turn, hold each elbow with the opposite hand and gently pull the elbow behind your head. Hold for 15 seconds (figure 5, *a* and *b*).

5   **Triceps extension stretch from the (a) front and (b) back.**

A Word About the Book's Structure

Between the covers, this book contains rock-solid information, precise instructions, and clear photos and illustrations to immerse you in the sport of archery. The bulk of the information is broken down into four sections:

- *You can do it:* Get a clear explanation of how to perform an essential skill or tactic.
- *More to choose and use:* Find out more and explore alternatives.
- *Take it to the range:* Apply the new skill in a hands-on situation.
- *Give it a go:* Use a drill or activity to hone or expand the fundamental techniques outlined in the chapter.

Apply the techniques and tactics as you learn them, and have fun!

Bows

How do you select the right bow for you? First, it's important to note that archery is a sport of storing and releasing energy in a controlled and hopefully consistent fashion. The bow, when drawn back, stores energy in its limbs that it then transfers to the arrow when you release the string. For optimal safety, performance, and speed, the bow must be the correct size for you, taking into account your height, strength, and dexterity, and whether you are right- or left-handed. Bow manufacturers compensate for a variety of body types by making bows in many sizes. This chapter outlines the parts of the bow and describes how to select the correct archery equipment for you, based on your physical traits and needs.

Before You Buy

Bows come in the following three basic styles:

- *Longbow:* The longbow is usually made from a single stick of material. It is straight when unstrung and forms a simple backward curve when strung.

- *Recurve bow:* Similar to the style of bow shot in the Olympic Games, the recurve bow has elongated limbs that, when strung, curve backward near the riser and then curve forward (recurve) at the tips. This bow has a smoother draw and release than a longbow does.

- *Compound bow:* The compound bow is a shorter and more compact bow that was originally invented for hunting but is now immensely popular among competitive archers. It features a series of wheels, cams, cables, and strings. A cam is a special type of wheel that creates greater bow speed than a round wheel does.

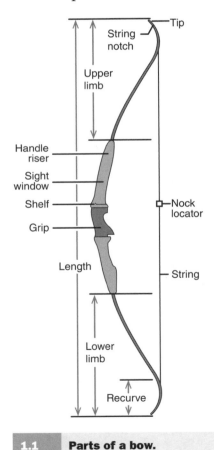

1.1 **Parts of a bow.**

Although bows differ in looks depending on what they're used for, they all have some basic traits in common. When strung, all bows are bent in some fashion. The center part of the bow that you hold with your bow hand is called the riser, or the handle.

A bowstring, which connects the limbs, is often made of a series of synthetic fibers that are protected by special reinforced thread at the ends and the center called servings. The center serving often has a small brass ring or wound thread on it called a nock locator. The nock locator is positioned onto the serving on a specific spot, below or between where the notched back part of the arrow (called the nock) snaps onto the string (figure 1.1).

Commonly thought of as the bow used by Robin Hood and featured in countless Hollywood movies, the longbow is a simple, straight piece of carved wood with a string. Longbows have no additional components (e.g., sights, arrow rests). Originating in Europe, the longbow was made from a variety of local wood, including yew. When archery started to become popular in America, Osage orange became a popular wood for bow makers, who are also called bowyers. Currently, hickory, lemonwood, and bamboo are popular materials for longbow construction.

A recurve bow has elongated limbs above and below the riser that have a lengthy curve, and the string is connected at the very end of the limb, called the limb tip. A compound bow has a distinct riser and upper and lower limbs that are less curved than their recurve bow counterparts. On a compound bow, the string makes the connection to the bow at the wheels or cams. The cam is attached to the tip of one or both limbs.

Found on the riser is a cutout called a sight window. The lower part of the sight window, called the shelf, can act as the direct place on the bow on which the arrow rests while the bow is being drawn. This is frequently found on fiberglass bows and longbows. The sight window may also have holes drilled in it with metal inserts for a small arm—called a rest—that holds the arrow. Some arrow rests have self-adhesive pads so they can be stuck onto the side of the sight window. The sight window may also have drilled inserts that accept mounts for a wide variety of aiming aids called sights. Bow sights are usually made of metal or plastic, and they have an adjustable aperture (recurve bow) or magnified scope (compound bow) used for aiming.

Bows come in a variety of draw lengths and draw weights. Draw length is the distance you pull the bow back when you draw it fully and the string is at the correct location at the corner of your mouth or under your chin (called the anchor point). Draw length is measured from the front of the arrow rest on the bow to the front of the inside of the nock on the arrow. Draw length differs from person to person based on body type and shooting technique (figure 1.2). Draw weight is the amount of pull the bow exerts at your full draw length. Recurve bows and compound bows differ slightly in how draw length functions. On a recurve bow, because everyone has a slightly different draw length, the draw weight differs slightly. The farther back you pull a recurve bow, the more energy it stores in the limbs, and the heavier it draws. However, an industry standard states that the advertised draw weight of a bow, which is usually printed on the bottom bow limb, is meant for a 28-inch (71 cm) draw length.

1.2   **Draw length.**

On a compound bow, draw length is preset by a module on the cam that limits the length the bow can be drawn back, in order to have the draw stop at your anchor point. Some cams allow the draw length to be adjusted by changing or moving modules, while others require a complete cam change to change draw length. In either case, these adjustments can be made at your local archery shop. The cam allows you to pull the bow back to the proper draw length using the full draw weight of the bow; at the end of the draw, the cam rotates to lessen the holding weight of the bow (an action called let-off)—allowing you to hold the bow back at full draw at just a fraction of its original draw weight. Additionally, most compound bows have approximately a 10-pound (4.5 kg) draw weight range, although some bows have a greater range. The weight is easily adjusted at a pro shop.

More to choose and use

SELECTING A BOW

What's the right bow for you? The answer depends on how you intend to use it. Archers usually decide what kind of archery appeals to them and then choose the equipment that best matches that goal.

Some archers eventually own several types of bows. Compound archers can benefit from shooting a recurve, and vice versa; each type of bow teaches technique lessons. For tournaments and games, the equipment must be the same or similar for archers within a given category to compete fairly with one another. Following are some common types of bows and their suggested uses.

Longbow   Longbows are still very popular with archers who like the traditional feel and style of an all-wood bow (figure 1.3, *a* and *b*). The bows are carefully carved so that the limbs draw back evenly. The grip is often a wrapped strip of leather. The arrow rests either on the back of the archer's gloved hand or on a narrow shelf carefully cut into the bow above the grip. Today's longbows can be beautiful works of art, highly prized by their makers and owners. Longbows, like recurve and compound bows, are equally appropriate for beginners and experienced archers. As with all bows, it is recommended that the archer work with a coach or expert at a local archery shop to select a bow that suits his or her goals and body type.

1.3   *(a)* **Longbow and** *(b)* **shooting with a longbow.**

Recurve Bow: One-Piece and Takedown The modern recurve, also called the Olympic recurve, is an improvement over the longbow in that the limbs and riser are built to store and conduct energy more efficiently. Also, they apply greater speed and power to the arrow. Recurve bows are common in target and field archery, and they are the only bows allowed in the Olympic Games (figure 1.4). Some recurve bows are made in one piece and resemble the longbow except for their recurved limbs. A one-piece recurve bow can be made from laminated wood and synthetics. This one-piece bow has a very small handle, or riser. The small riser allows the limbs to also be shorter, making the bow easier to handle in the field. A one-piece recurve bow is often considered a traditional bow, owing to its appearance, and is used for bowhunting or for competitive archery. The Olympic recurve bow, on the other hand, is often approximately the height of the archer when unstrung, and is made in three pieces: upper limb, lower limb, and riser.

To make the recurve bow more portable, the takedown bow was created. This type of bow separates into a riser and two limbs. The riser is most often 23 or 25 inches (58 or 64 cm) long, although 21- and 27-inch (53 and 69 cm) variations are available from some manufacturers. The limbs are often made of wood, fiberglass, carbon, foam, or

1.4 **Recurve bow.**

a combination thereof. Almost all currently made competition-grade recurve bows are takedown bows because of their portability. These bows are also designed to accommodate a variety of accessories to maximize the performance of the bow, lend it greater stability, and help the archer to aim. The design engineering and manufacturing quality of top-level competition recurve bows continue to progress from season to season.

Compound Bow Compound bows are lean, mean archery machines (figure 1.5). With limbs, cams, and mechanical wheels, compound bows allow you to add the advantage of technology to your archery skill—although no amount of technology will compensate for practice with whatever bow you choose. As mentioned before, with a longbow or a recurve, the farther back you draw the bow, the more weight you pull, because the bow weight increases with draw length. A compound bow stores energy in the limb while the bow is drawn; it then "lets off" the pulling weight as the draw length is reached, thanks to a rotating cam on one or more of the limbs. Imagine holding and aiming a bow at full draw while holding a fraction of the weight—that's what shooting a compound bow feels like. The primary advantages are the ease of holding the bow back longer for aiming, and the ability to use accessories to balance the lighter holding weight with the mass weight of the bow.

1.5 **Compound bow.**

Opinions vary as to whether archers should learn the sport with a compound bow. Most coaches recommend starting with a recurve bow to learn the basics, but the reality is that compound bows are extremely popular, and many archers start with them. If you are a beginning archer, more important than the type of bow you choose is that you get good coaching from a certified instructor or coach, and purchase a bow personally fitted to you from a reputable pro shop. Don't start on a compound bow just because it's given to you, you found it at a tag sale, or you purchased it without consultation. Remember that a compound bow achieves its unique performance by being properly sized and fitted for your particular draw length and dexterity and the appropriate draw weight for your strength and skill level. Because each of us has a unique draw length, a compound bow must be fitted to your body type and size. Pulling a compound bow that isn't properly fitted (i.e., is too heavy, overdrawn, or undersized) can result in physical injury—sometimes serious.

Highly Adjustable Compound Bow

A popular trend in compound bow design is to make youth bows that are adjustable from very short draw lengths to adult-sized draw lengths (figure 1.6). This allows the bow to grow with the archer, which is more cost effective than buying new bows for growing archers. For adult archers, many compound bows offer ranges of adjustment as well. For those who are uncertain about whether to use compound bows with beginning archers, one bow manufacturer—Mathews—has created and patented a small, light-draw-weight compound bow called the Genesis that does not have a let-off like other compounds. This bow's cam draws back like a recurve but with a steady draw weight that doesn't increase. As a result, archers of varying draw lengths can use the same bow. And because the bow has light-draw-weight options, beginning archers are less likely to strain themselves while learning proper form. One of the primary reasons people encourage beginners to use recurve bows is that they believe learning to release with the fingers (versus a mechanical release aid on a compound) teaches better archery fun-

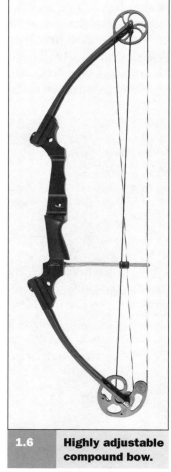

1.6 **Highly adjustable compound bow.**

Courtesy of Mathews, Inc.

damentals that prepare archers to shoot whichever type of bow they choose. However, the Genesis allows archers to set the bow up like a compound or a recurve, so they can shoot with their fingers and eventually graduate to a mechanical release aid.

When you're just starting out, it's always better to start with a simple, lightweight bow that is properly fitted than it is to go with a poorly fitting heavy bow that will decrease your enjoyment of the sport and possibly overpower or injure you.

Take it to the range

Buying a Compound or Recurve Bow

There are lots of options in a compound bow, and each offers its own advantages. Some bows offer solid limb technology; others come in split limb variations (figure 1.7). Two-cam or cam-and-a-half bows offer two cams or a cam plus a cam–wheel hybrid; other bows offer a single cam and an idler wheel. Whatever type of compound bow you purchase, know that you're joining millions of archers who have discovered the fun of compound shooting. Whether at a field, at a 3D (three-dimensional) or target archery tournament, bowhunting, or just shooting arrows for fun in the backyard, the compound bow offers a fun challenge for everyone.

When you are buying a recurve bow, there are a few important characteristics to look for. Consider the dexterity, length, and draw weight of the bow. Think about where you are in your development as an archer. For example, if this is your first recurve bow, you might consider purchasing an inexpensive takedown recurve with wood limbs and a wood riser that is meant for entry-level target shooting. You could invest in an aluminum or carbon riser, but

1.7 Split limb compound bow.

make sure you start with an entry-level set of limbs, because you are likely to go through a set of limbs or two before you arrive at the proper draw weight.

The most important accessory for a recurve bow is the bowstring. Bowstring measurements are needed for safety and for best performance. First, the string must be the proper length as listed on your bow. Be sure you are reading the correct measurement: The total length of your recurve bow is the sum of the riser length and the limb length. For example, some limbs read *30# at 66*, and below that, *32# at 64*. What those two lines mean is that these limbs will make a 30-pound (14 kg), 66-inch (168 cm) bow when put on a 25-inch (63.5 cm) riser, and a 32-pound (14.5 kg), 64-inch (162.5 cm) bow if put on a 23-inch (58 cm) riser. The string will need to be made for the length of the bow you have, so be sure to bring your bow with you to the pro shop if you're not certain of the measurement (figure 1.8). They can take a measurement for you.

The center serving must be the proper diameter to snugly fit the nocks on your arrows. Anytime you change either the bowstring or

1.8 A knowledgeable expert such as a coach or retailer can evaluate the fit of your recurve bow.

the arrows, always double-check that the fit is still snug between the bowstring and the nock. You can tell this is the case if the nock snaps onto the string without using any real force. If the fit is too tight, the arrow will not release smoothly. And if the fit is too loose, the arrow will constantly fall off the string prior to release, which creates a safety and performance concern.

Bowstrings are made by looping a single strand of fiber around specially made pieces of metal—called a string jig—multiple times. On the bowstring packaging, you will see not only the bowstring length but also the number of strands with which it's made. This number is always even. Generally, the more strands a string has, the heavier the bow is for which it is intended. A common beginner bowstring for a lightweight bow with 20 pounds (9 kg) of draw weight will have 10 to 12 strands, depending on the bowstring material. Remember to always double-check to see if the nocks of your arrows fit snugly into the bowstring before shooting. Again, if in doubt, be sure to get advice from an instructor, coach, or professional at a local retail archery shop.

Buying Used Equipment

When you're starting out in archery, you might find good used equipment if you shop carefully with an eye for safety and aren't afraid to walk away from a questionable deal. A great way to look for used equipment is through your local archery retailer or pro shop, because they have trained salespeople who can ensure that the bow fits you correctly. Match the equipment to your ability and physical size (lighter is better), and ask someone knowledgeable about archery (again, the local retailer is a good start) to inspect the bow for damage or safety flaws. The expert should ensure that the bow limbs draw back straight without twisting and have no signs of delaminating or shredding (separating) layers. All mounting bolts or threaded inserts should be intact, and the handle should fit comfortably in your hand without forcing you into an uncomfortable position. Any accessories should fit properly onto the bow.

Do not purchase equipment that needs to be repaired. Even some of the most experienced archers trust their equipment to mechanical experts at a pro shop rather than fix it themselves. Fixing broken equipment is a job for an expert, and repairs left undone by beginning archers (a common occurrence) can lead to serious injury. If money is an issue, it's always better to purchase a less expensive new bow suitable for you from a knowledgeable retailer.

DETERMINING YOUR DRAW HAND

For many years, conventional wisdom held that archers draw the bow with the hand on the same side as their dominant eye. People would do a simple eye dominance test using their interlocked hands to see which eye did most of the work; they would then use the hand on that side for drawing the bow. However, in recent years, coaches have discovered that it's often more effective to ask the archer which hand he or she uses for throwing a ball or doing other physical activities, and then recommend that the archer start by using that hand to draw the bow. It's usually easier to teach an archer to close the opposite eye than it is to develop muscle coordination and strength on the side of the body that isn't often used. So, to determine whether to use your right or left hand to draw the bow, ask yourself which hand you would use to throw a ball or swing a tennis racket, or (if you're not athletically inclined) which hand you write with. That is the hand you should start using to draw the bow.

INSTALLING AN ARROW REST

Recurve and compound bows must have an arrow rest installed, in good working condition, to shoot safely and correctly. An arrow rest may be a simple, nonadjustable stick-on variety, or it may be adjustable. Arrow rests can vary widely in cost and material. As a smart beginning archer who is starting out by focusing on the basics, your best bet is a stick-on arrow rest (figure 1.9). A stick-on rest is positioned on the sight window, directly above the shelf of the bow. This rest safely holds the arrow in place while you are drawing back and releasing.

To install a stick-on rest, first scrape away any remaining glue or adhesive from the bow handle from any previous rest if the bow is used. You can do this

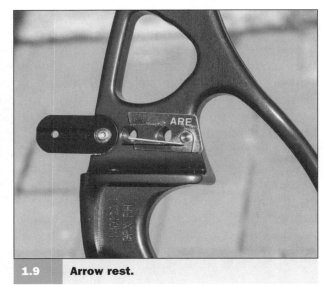

1.9   **Arrow rest.**

by gently using a razor blade, although be extra careful if the riser is made of wood or painted, as opposed to anodized. Clean the area where the new adhesive pad will stick on, using acetone or lacquer thinner (but be sure to use adequate ventilation). Remove the adhesive backing on the arrow rest, and position it directly above the shelf. In many cases, the bow will have a circular insert hole drilled into the riser directly above the shelf, and the rest will have a corresponding hole molded into it. Align both holes and ensure that the rest is horizontal relative to the shelf. Once the rest is in the correct position, press down firmly to attach it to the riser.

INSTALLING A NOCK LOCATOR

Only after you have positioned the arrow rest should you take this next step. All bows must have a nock locator attached to the bowstring. The nock locator acts as a reference point to ensure that the arrow is nocked on the bow in the same position shot after shot. It is also a safety feature to prevent the nock from traveling up and down the string. Nock locators (also called nocking points) are tiny open rings, often made of soft brass, that have an interior lining of rubber to grip the string without cutting it. Special pliers, called nockset pliers, are used for installing and removing nock locators.

To install the nock locator, first string your bow (see the procedure in chapter 4). Then place the accessory called a bow square (sometimes called a T-square) onto the arrow rest, with the long piece placed on the arrow rest and the *T* part clipped all the way onto the bowstring (figure 1.10). The bow square measures right angles to

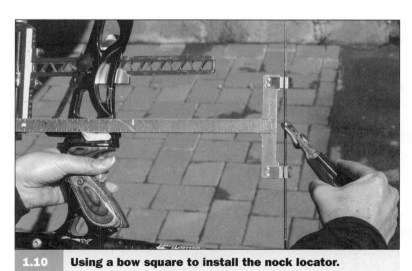

1.10   **Using a bow square to install the nock locator.**

position the nock locator properly on the bowstring. The back of the bow square has a small ruler. Position the bottom of the nock locator 3/8 of an inch (about 1 cm) above horizontal and clip it onto the bowstring using nockset pliers (or regular pliers). Squeeze firmly in several directions to get an even fit onto the bowstring.

On Target

Whether you decide on a compound, recurve, or longbow, remember that lighter is always better. For the recurve, select one that is about the same height as you are and no more than 20 pounds (9 kg) in draw weight. If you start with a compound bow, it must be properly fitted specifically to you and be easy to draw back—20 to 30 pounds (9 to 14 kg), or even lighter if needed. Make sure your bow has a new bowstring and a properly positioned arrow rest and nock locator. If you select a longbow, you won't be using an arrow rest because you'll shoot the arrow directly off the shelf of the bow, but you will need a new bowstring and a nock locator installed. You can buy inexpensive bow squares, nockset pliers, nock locators, and bowstrings from your local archery retailer—and even if you have them do the installation for you, you can ask questions and learn from their expertise.

Arrows

Arrows, which are as significant to your shot as the bow, have unique characteristics and should be purchased with care. Arrows differ in length, weight, and flexibility, and they should be matched according to your bow and the type of archery you'll be shooting. The right arrow can complement your shot perfectly, and the wrong arrow can make your bow unsafe to shoot.

Your first concern is the length of the arrow. For you to be able to draw the bow back safely, the arrow must be long enough that its point extends at least a full 2 inches (5 cm) beyond the front of the riser when you have reached your correct anchor point. Experienced archers may use arrows slightly shorter than this; however, beginners, who tend to take some time to find their proper anchor point and upper-body alignment, should use the 2-inch (5 cm) guideline for safety's sake.

Target archers using recurve bows tend to favor slender, lightweight arrows with small fletchings (vanes or feathers) for greater range and lessened wind resistance. As a rule, most target archers use feathers for indoor shooting (although vanes work just as well in many cases) and vanes for outdoor shooting, where wind can be a factor. Compound archers tend to favor stiffer, larger-diameter arrows with vanes for outdoor shooting and feathers or vanes that produce the best possible flight for indoor shooting. When starting out, the most important thing to remember—more so than the type of fletching on the arrow—is that the length of the arrow must be appropriate to your draw length. The arrow must also flex properly when leaving the bow.

The desired flexibility, or spine, of an arrow is calculated based on several variables, particularly draw weight and draw length. This chapter discusses these variables. The arrows you shoot on any given day should ideally be identical: the same length, spine, brand, and style; the same fletching, point type, and weight; and the same nocks and fletchings. Only then will you be capable of shooting consistent groups.

You can do it

Purchasing Arrows

You can acquire the proper arrows for your bow by buying finished arrows (figure 2.1) or by building them yourself. Buying arrows that are already assembled is the easiest and most productive route for beginning archers. Arrow manufacturers generally make a broad range of arrows and provide selection charts that allow you to easily match your bow and shooting style to the arrows they sell. Some mail-order companies offer finished arrows in their retail catalogs, which is helpful if you already know what kind of finished arrows you need. Mail-order arrows might be the cheapest—but if you order the wrong size or spine, you may find they are not returnable.

2.1   **Assortment of preassembled arrows.**

Visit the websites of many popular arrow manufacturers; nearly all of them have arrow selection charts that allow you to use your draw length and draw weight to determine the correct spine for you. Certain variables determine the arrow spine you need. Arrow selection charts typically consist of grids with arrow types and spines in each square. Columns on either side of the grid refer to draw weight, arrow length, whether you are shooting a compound or recurve bow, and the type of compound cam.

The best route if you are a beginning archer is to visit your local pro shop. There you can be professionally measured for draw weight and draw length, and have arrows made specifically for you that work with your bow.

The first step is to determine the draw weight of your bow. Be sure you know the particular weight *you* are drawing, and not just the weight noted on the bow. That number typically describes a range that is measured at a certain draw length, which may or may not apply to you, depending on your body type. The best and most accurate way to determine draw weight, which directly correlates to the spine of arrow you will need, is to have it measured by a certified coach or an archery retailer. These professionals use a bow scale to measure the weight you are pulling at your particular draw length (figure 2.2).

The next step in using the arrow chart to determine the arrow type and spine you need is to find your draw length. This, too, should be determined with the help of your local retailer or your archery coach.

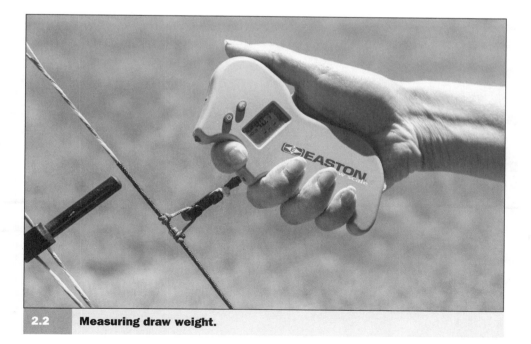

2.2 **Measuring draw weight.**

Once you've determined your draw length and weight, it's time to go back to the arrow selection chart. Locate where the draw-length column meets the draw-weight row. This square lists one or more arrow types and spines that should work for you. The draw length is printed on the manufacturer label (figure 2.3).

Your local archery retailer will help you choose the proper arrow and order them or make them up for you, if they are in stock. Making the arrows involves determining the fletchings that are needed, the type and weight of the point, and the type of nock, if one is not already installed.

Your retailer will generally hold off on cutting the arrow shafts to your size and gluing in the points until you've had a chance to remeasure the arrow in your bow (without shooting it). Your retailer or coach will install the proper nocks for your arrow shaft (including a metal pin under the nock, if the arrow calls for it), and then have you draw the arrow back to ensure the correct length. This is done by comparing the length of the arrow shaft with the draw length and the location of the arrow point in relation to the arrow rest. The arrow may need to be trimmed back a bit to make it the proper length for you. Length, weight, and spine are all directly interrelated, so it's important to have the help of your certified coach or retailer when determining how to cut and point your arrows. Once they are cut and pointed for you, they are most likely not returnable and could be difficult to resell if it turns out they are the wrong length for you.

2.3 **Bow weight and draw length printed on the manufacturer label.**

ARROW COMPONENTS

All arrows, in spite of cosmetic and design differences, have similar components (figure 2.4). The body of the arrow is called the shaft. The point is the metal front end. The point may be glued onto the outside of the shaft (which is usually the case with wood or fiberglass arrows) or can be glued on by inserting it into the shaft. Points for aluminum, carbon, and composite arrows are typically inserted into the arrow shaft. For points that may need to be removed in the future, as is the case for most target archers, a special type of hot-melt glue is used to insert the points. Your coach or retailer will use a propane torch to heat the glue gently, because this type of glue has a low melting point. The shank (or long back part) of the point is then coated in glue, and the shank is inserted into the arrow shaft. Excess glue is wiped off, and the arrow is set aside to cool. One of the major reasons for getting professional help with making arrows until you are an experienced archer is that heat can be very damaging to most types of arrow shafts. Experience is needed to properly heat glue onto points and avoid heating the shaft and permanently damaging the arrow.

A design (or a manufacturer's logo) called the crest is often placed on the arrow shaft. On most aluminum, carbon, and composite arrows, this crest is in the form of a very thin decal that is permanently put onto the arrow during the manufacturing process. Traditional archers making wooden arrows also often crest their arrows, but with paint. Target, field, and 3D archers may also use decorative wraps to crest their arrows.

Fletchings are three feathers or three soft, thin plastic vanes that are glued onto the shaft with a special type of glue, depending on the composition of the arrow. The end of the arrow opposite the point is capped with a notched nock, which engages the bowstring. Nocks may be glued over the arrow shaft or inserted into it. In either case, it is important to line up the nock correctly with the fletchings—the

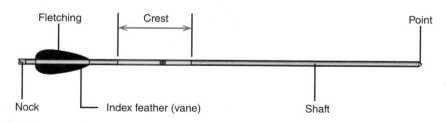

Fletching   Crest   Point

Nock   Index feather (vane)   Shaft

2.4   **Parts of an arrow.**

upright vanes or feathers glued onto the back of the arrow. The fletching that is lined up with the nock depends on the type of bow and type of arrow rest being used. Most arrows have a three-vane or three-feather fletching, and one of the vanes or feathers is often a different color from the other two. This third vane or feather, called the index vane or index feather, faces away from the shelf of a recurve bow when the arrow is nocked on the string, and may face up or down on a compound bow depending on the type of arrow rest used. Check this before the nock is inserted, especially if it will be glued into place. Again, there is no substitute for archery knowledge and experience, so ask your coach or local retailer for help with this.

SPINE

The degree of stiffness or weakness in an arrow (i.e., the amount of flex in the arrow shaft) is referred to as the spine. Several variables affect spine, including the material from which the arrow is made, the thickness of the wall of the arrow shaft, the diameter and length of the arrow shaft, and the weights of the various arrow parts (nock, point). The length of the arrow shaft, as well as the draw weight of the bow, greatly affects how much the arrow flexes. Advanced archers will even change bowstring type, the number of strands on a bowstring, nock types, and other variables to obtain the best flexibility from the arrow. This is also referred to as the way the bow and arrow *tune*. The numbers on the arrow selection chart, aside from identifying the arrow you want to buy, tell a great deal about the shaft of the arrow in terms of shaft diameter and wall thickness.

Think of each number as two sets of two-digit numbers. The first two digits indicate the shaft diameter in 64ths of an inch. The second two digits indicate the wall thickness in 1,000ths of an inch. It follows then that you can select an arrow based on both wall thickness and diameter to achieve proper spine. The arrow selection chart provides some spine options, but fine-tuning will need to happen with the help of someone experienced who can counsel you about achieving an even better "bow tune" using point weight, nocks, and so forth, to achieve the desired amount of flex in the arrow.

SHAFT COMPOSITION

Arrows have been made from almost any material you can imagine. From simple river reeds to highly engineered composites, arrow makers and archers are constantly experimenting with materials and designs, and arrows continue to become faster and more efficient as technology evolves. The four basic material groupings are wood, fiberglass, aluminum, and carbon. Composite arrows typically involve some combination of aluminum and carbon (figure 2.5).

Wood is the traditional arrow material. The preferred wood for making arrows tends to be cedar—it's inexpensive, knot free, and fairly straight, and it has a pretty even grain for consistency. Cedar arrows are prone to breaking under high bow weights or from striking a hard target, however, and they can warp due to humidity. However, wood is still favored by some traditional archers who make their own arrows and enjoy the authenticity of wood.

Fiberglass arrows are often used in archery programs because they are straight, durable, and relatively inexpensive. These arrows are good for programs in which the quantity of equipment is more important than accuracy. Care must be taken to inspect fiberglass arrows frequently and cautiously for slivers or splitting.

Aluminum arrows are quite common among tournament archers. In target archery, aluminum shafts are favored for indoor shooting, where archers may gain a slight advantage as a result of the generally larger diameter of aluminum arrows. However, many archers also find success using aluminum arrows outdoors at shorter distances. Aluminum shafts come in a wide variety of spines, colors, and price ranges. If bent, they often can be straightened and reused.

Carbon arrows are made from carbon filaments running down the length of the arrow. Known for their straightness and thin diameter, carbon arrows have less wind resistance than thicker arrows made from other materials and so tend to maintain their velocity better at longer ranges. These shafts are especially popular among 3D

2.5 Shafts of various compositions: aluminum, wood, carbon, fiberglass, and carbon and aluminum composite.

archers and bowhunters. Carbon arrows should always be inspected for loose slivers or splitting prior to shooting.

Finally, composite arrows, although not really a single material, represent the cutting edge of arrow technology. Aluminum and carbon are bonded together in layers to take advantage of both materials' characteristics. These composite "super-arrows" are often found on the bows of the best archers in the world, at the Olympic and Paralympic Games, and at outdoor World Championship events. However, you should choose your arrows based on what works best for your individual setups, rather than on what top archers are using.

NOCK

The nock, although small, plays a vital role in properly holding the arrow on the bowstring. The rear notch of the nock snaps onto the center serving of the bowstring just below the nocking point, and holds the arrow firmly on the bowstring (figure 2.6). Some nock manufacturers mold in a slight bump inside the notch that clicks onto the string. Not only must the nock fit firmly on the bowstring, but it must also release the arrow easily when you release the bowstring to shoot the arrow.

In general, you should feel the arrow snap onto the bowstring. When taking the arrow off the string by hand, there should be some resistance, but it should not be difficult to remove. Nocks are made differently for different types of arrow shafts and archery applications. Your local archery pro shop should have a supply of nocks

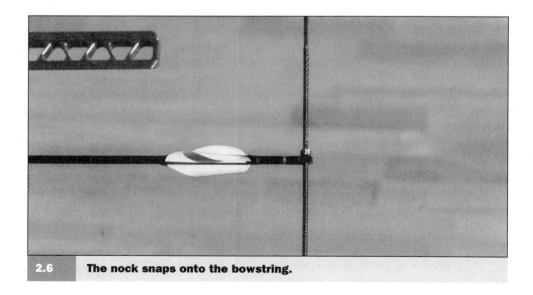

2.6   **The nock snaps onto the bowstring.**

of various sizes to choose from, to replace the ones on your arrows if needed. The most important quality in a nock is that it's in good condition and free of cracks, splinters, and gouges. Even if the nock snaps onto the string, a visual inspection is always in order to be sure it is making proper contact with the bowstring.

FLETCHING

The arrow is steered in flight by its fletching—the upright vanes or feathers glued onto the back of the arrow. The index vane or index feather positions the arrow properly on the arrow rest to allow the arrow to clear the rest and cushion plunger, if one is installed. The fletching steers the arrow by acting as a rudder and providing wind resistance at the rear—keeping the front of the flying arrow pointing toward the target. The best fletching for any shooting situation maximizes stability while minimizing drag.

Fletchings are made from either soft plastic (vanes) or from feathers harvested from turkeys or other birds. They come in a wide variety of shapes, sizes, and colors. In the past, target arrows tended to have smaller vanes, and hunting arrows tended to have larger ones. However, today, hunters have very short and small vane options, and target archers sometimes use longer feathers for indoor archery (for more stability) and smaller vanes for outdoor archery (for optimal wind performance). Fletching length is somewhat related to arrow length in that a longer arrow is better stabilized by a 4-inch (10 cm) feather than a 3-inch (7.6 cm) feather, for example. As a rule, longer fletchings add stability but increase drag, slowing the arrow down. In general, it's important to get some help setting up your arrows for the specific archery game you will be playing. Fletchings will perform differently indoors, outdoors, and at varying distances.

Feathers are very popular, and they are still one of the best choices for fletching materials (figure 2.7). Feathers provide more drag on an arrow and so help stabilize it better than plastic vanes, which provide less drag. Feathers are softer and collapse downward when touched, which lessens snagging while coming off the arrow rest or when in contact with other bow parts.

The base of a feather fletching isn't symmetrical in the way a plastic vane is. Feathers are referred to as right wing or left wing based on the side of the bird from which they are harvested. Feathers from either wing are equally accurate; just be sure that the same side wing feathers are used on a single arrow. Using wing feathers from both sides on a single arrow could create very unstable arrow flight.

Vanes stabilize the arrow in several ways at the same time. They steer the arrow like a rudder; provide drag on the arrow to keep the

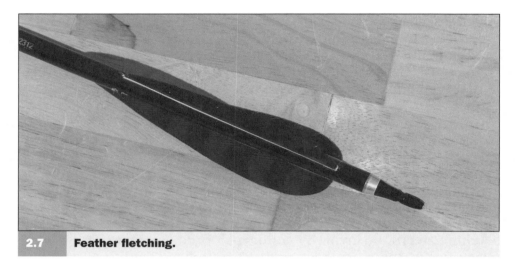

2.7 Feather fletching.

front pointed toward the target; and often are set at a slight angle, called an offset, which provides added stability by spinning the arrow on its axis as it flies. For accuracy and stability, it doesn't matter in which direction the arrow spins.

CREST

Cresting has its roots in ancient archery, when archers' arrows could be identified by their family crests. Today, cresting is used by manufacturers both aesthetically and practically: to make arrows more attractive and to designate the brand, model, and size or spine of the arrow. Many traditional archers still take the time to paint cresting on their arrows, and the results can be quite artistic and beautiful. Crests can be handy for identifying your arrows at tournaments or when shooting with other archers who have the same fletching colors as you. Plus, it's fun to create colorful stripes and designs. You can also have fun with arrow wraps—a modern version of cresting—which we cover later in this chapter.

POINTS

Arrow points break down the spine of the arrow by increasing the amount of flex in the arrow shaft, and most basically, points are what make the arrow stick into the target. They can be long, short, sharp, or rounded (figure 2.8); the possibilities are seemingly endless. The point may be capped over the arrow shaft, as on fiberglass arrows, or inserted into a hollow arrow shaft and glued with hot glue or in-

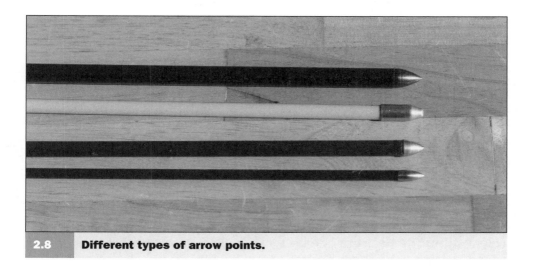

Different types of arrow points.

stant cyanoacrylate (CA) glue, as on arrows used for target archery. Many bowhunters favor field points for practicing. In this case, an insert is glued into the arrow shaft; a field point can be screwed into the insert for practice and then unscrewed if the bowhunter wants to substitute a hunting point (called a broadhead). Points can be purchased separately from arrows, and they are available in various weights and lengths. Because the arrow point weighs very little, special scales are used, and the unit of measure is grains. One pound (0.5 kg) is the approximate equivalent of 7,000 grains.

Take it to the range

Archer's Paradox

Many recreational archers decide to buy only finished arrows based on the selection charts that manufacturers provide. That's fine, but archery is a sport of science. Knowing why an arrow behaves the way it does is important if you want to choose or create the perfect arrow for you.

A paradox is a statement or concept that contains conflicting ideas. The archer's paradox refers to the fact that an arrow may look as though it's stiff and flying perfectly straight when it's actually wiggling, or oscillating, in flight. If you could watch the arrow in super slow motion, you would see that although it appears to be traveling in a straight path, it is actually bending back and forth like a wet noodle. The arrow oscillates around two balance points called nodes—one toward the front and one toward the back of the arrow.

When an arrow is released from a bow, the bowstring acts like an engine pushing the arrow along. As the arrow is leaving the bow but still in contact with the bowstring, it's accelerating. Because the push of the bowstring is coming from the rear, the rear is trying to move faster than the front of the arrow, which causes the arrow to wiggle in flight. The arrow shaft has a specific inherent stiffness to it that is precalibrated by the manufacturer. This inherent stiffness eventually slows the arrow's wiggle in flight, and the arrow begins to stabilize as it gets closer to the target. The archer's paradox, in fact, becomes a balance between the side-to-side wiggle of the arrow and the dampening effect of its own stiffness. A certain amount of wiggle is desired because it absorbs some of the initial shock of being released suddenly from the bowstring. Too much stiffness, and the arrow could strike the side of the bow handle upon release and fly off course. Conversely, too much weakness—the term archers use for excess flexibility in the arrow—and the arrow will wiggle too much in flight, again causing accuracy and range to suffer.

The type of bow and the way the bowstring is released also affect the archer's paradox. Arrows shot from a compound bow with a mechanical release aid tend to have a vertical flex. Arrows shot from a recurve bow but released from the bowstring with the fingers generally flex horizontally. In fact, an inconsistent release of the bowstring can alter the way arrows shot from the same recurve bow flex, effectively altering the paradox.

In choosing the proper arrow, you are actually trying to strike a balance between an arrow that's stiff enough to take advantage of the thrust of the bowstring, yet flexible enough to ensure proper flight and accuracy. The arrow selection chart is the manufacturer's attempt at making educated guesses on your shooting requirements, and, for the most part, they get pretty close. But advanced archers spend considerable time sampling arrow models and spines to find the ones that work best for them.

Give it a go

ARROW WRAPS

There are a few key ways to personalize your arrows, and a fun way is to add arrow wraps (figure 2.9). Arrow wraps of various designs can be purchased from your local archery pro shop. In fact, some companies even print custom wraps in almost any pattern you

2.9 Arrow wraps.

choose! One word of caution: If you have carefully tuned your bow, adding arrow wraps could slightly change the way the bow tunes. For beginner and intermediate archers, the difference will be very small, if any.

Be sure that the size of the wrap you are purchasing is appropriate for the size and diameter of your arrow. To apply an arrow wrap, first carefully clean the shaft with lacquer thinner and allow it to dry. Next, use a flat, even, but somewhat soft surface to apply the wraps (a mouse pad works well). Unpeel the arrow wrap from its backing, sticky side up. Line the arrow up carefully so that the edge of the wrap is lined up with where the nock meets the arrow shaft. Slowly roll the arrow shaft onto the wrap, taking care to do so evenly so that air bubbles don't form. Continue until the wrap is completely adhered to the arrow shaft (figure 2.10). Once you've done that, it's time to fletch your personalized arrows!

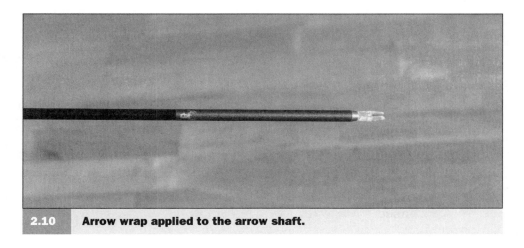

2.10 Arrow wrap applied to the arrow shaft.

On Target

In this chapter, you learned what makes an arrow fly and how to select the best arrow for the type of archery you'll be enjoying. Archery is a sport of consistency, so your arrows must be identical and kept in good repair. If you are a beginning archer, you should work with a professional to determine the right type and size of arrow. Purchase quality finished arrows and learn how to shoot accurately with them before trying to make your own arrows. Once you have learned the basics of shooting and are shooting consistently enough to gain points by customizing your equipment, you are ready to appreciate the benefits of making your own arrows.

Accessories

So far, we've concentrated on shooting techniques and basic equipment. For beginning archers, less is more—meaning the fewer variables you have to worry about in the beginning, the faster you'll learn the basics and be ready to move on. Archery accessories, once you're ready for them, can help you improve your shooting and your accuracy. You'll know you're ready for them when your groups are consistent in the target and you feel comfortable and strong with respect to your technique.

There's a difference between adding accessories to improve your shooting and overaccessorizing to the point where you are focused more on gadgets than on your shooting form. Avoid trying to buy better scores with new accessories. No accessory can match the value of putting in the time it takes to develop good form. You can purchase accessories to enhance your shooting and stay within your budget. Accessories such as rests, stabilizers, finger tabs, and other items can last a long time, so before you buy, check with your instructor or coach, and your local archery retailer, for their recommendations.

Archery accessories come in a wide variety of styles, features, colors, brands, and prices. We'll discuss a few in general terms in case you purchase an accessory that looks slightly different. Many bows come drilled and tapped to accept accessories. Despite the wide variety of accessories available, most, if not all, will fit onto your bow thanks to accepted industry standards, which determine screw and bolt sizes.

ARROW RESTS

The most common accessory is the arrow rest, which holds your arrow in position above the bow shelf. Rests can be as simple as a plastic stick-on variety or as advanced as a magnetic rest with metal arm; many other varieties are available as well (figure 3.1, *a* and *b*). The stick-on arrow rest combines two useful features. First, it correctly positions the arrow for a straightaway launch while allowing for free clearance of the feathers or vanes. Second, it keeps the arrow slightly away from the bow riser and acts as a shock absorber when the arrow is launched. Most beginner bows are sold with a basic arrow rest, but check on this when purchasing. Unless you are shooting traditional archery, an arrow rest is a necessity. If your bow does not have one, you'll need to purchase one.

3.1 **(a) Simple and (b) complex arrow rests.**

Competition-grade arrow rests differ in designs and features according to the manufacturer. They do, however, share a few common functions. Arrow rests position the arrow correctly for launch, may have some form of adjustment, and may fall away from the arrow upon launch—either by a magnet or mechanical-release swing arm. Some arrow rests are designed for specific draw weights, so read the manufacturer's product guidelines to be sure you're purchasing one that's appropriate for your equipment.

ARM GUARDS AND FINGER TABS

Arm guards and finger tabs (figure 3.2) are necessary personal protective equipment for recurve archers, and some compound archers

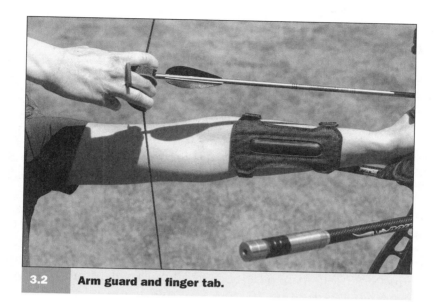

prefer wearing arm guards as well. An arm guard, whether for practice or competition, is a very simple accessory and does nothing more than keep the string from striking your arm or sleeve. Arm guards should always be worn when shooting a bow, although it is sometimes said that with proper shooting form the string will rarely hit your arm. If the string were to glance off your sleeve, it would also affect the consistent speed of the string and cause your accuracy to suffer. Arm guards can be attached with hooks and loops, snaps, or elastic bands and are often adjustable for arm size. Arm guards used for recreation might be made of plastic or leather and be wider than competition-style arm guards, which tend to be made of plastic or metal and are available in lots of styles and colors.

A finger tab keeps your fingers from being blistered by the bowstring, and it greatly aids in keeping your fingers in proper position on the string. A simple tab is generally punched out of leather and has a finger hole in the center for your middle finger to slide through. The tab may have a separator that separates your index finger from the rest of your fingers with a slot to accommodate the arrow nock. This helps you to form the correct hook, while preventing nock pinch. Competition-grade finger tabs may include various adjustments to better fit your hand, and they may also feature a top shelf to use against your lower jaw as an anchoring aid. There are numerous options for finger tabs in terms of the fit, the style, the type of metal, the weight of the tab itself, and the type of leather (some grades allow for a smoother string release than others). Regardless of the options it may have, any new tab, like a baseball glove, requires a break-in period during which the leather molds to your hand and is broken in by the act of releasing the string. Fully breaking in a new tab can take several weeks, so purchase one well ahead of your next competition. It's also a good idea to have an identical spare finger tab that is also broken in once you begin competing, in case your tab is lost or damaged.

QUIVERS

Quivers generally fall into two main categories for archers who have their own equipment: bow quivers and side quivers. Bow quivers were generally invented to hold spare arrows right on the side of the bow during bowhunting (figure 3.3a). Although convenient for being out in the woods, bow quivers should not be used on target archery ranges because they interfere with the balance and function of the bow.

Side quivers hang from a belt or clip at your side (figure 3.3b). This form of quiver is common in competitions because you can safely carry the arrows at your side from one target to the next if need be. Most coaches and archers consider side quivers the safest type to

3.3 *(a)* Bow quiver and *(b)* side quiver.

use on a range. If you use a side quiver, you will not have to carry your arrows after retrieving them from the target, which provides a measure of safety. Side quivers can be simple tubes or beautiful leather or fabric creations with various pocket options for accessories. A quiver is usually a matter of personal choice, based on function and design.

SIGHTS

A sight acts as a point of reference while aiming. Sights are the most common accessory for a recurve or compound bow, other than an arrow rest. Even simple program bows can be made more accurate by adding a stick-on front sight made of a matchstick. Sights typically have an aperture, in the shape of a ring, or a sight pin with which to aim. When held up to the distant target, a sight allows your eye to center the bow with the target naturally. Sights can be fixed (nonadjustable) or highly adjustable and very precise for tournament use. Adjustable sights can move from side to side and up and down to account for both windage and distance. On many tournament-style compound bows, the sight includes a magnified lens, called a scope, and often a level as well. Lenses are not permitted on recurve bows; recurve archers aim with the aperture or pin. Aperture, scope, lens, and pin options range from the type of magnification used in a scope, to the color of the ring in a recurve aperture, to whether or not to use a fiber optic pin. For advice on which option is best for you, consult your certified archery instructor or coach, who can relate this equipment purchase to your particular shooting technique. (Chapter 7 includes detailed information on mounting and using sights.)

PLUNGERS AND STABILIZERS

A plunger is an adjustable spring inside a threaded housing that screws into the bow's riser and comes out through the hole in the arrow rest (figure 3.4). It keeps the arrow in proper position on the arrow rest for release. The plunger also prevents the arrow from hitting the bow as it is released from the bowstring. It literally provides a cushion for the arrow to flex against as it leaves the bow. The plunger has two means of adjustment: moving it in or out of the threaded hole to adjust the center shot, and increasing or decreasing the spring tension, which changes the way the arrow flexes.

A properly adjusted plunger keeps the arrow in line with the bowstring in what is called center shot. In center shot, as you look down the shaft of the arrow after it's nocked onto the bowstring, back to front, you'll see that the arrow tip is slightly outside the center of the bowstring. When you release the bowstring with your fingers, a slight sideways effect occurs as the string rolls off your fingertips. This initial center-shot position is intended to counter the sideways effect on the arrow as it leaves the bow. The plunger keeps the arrow from hitting the side of the bow as it's released, which results in less side-to-side motion of the arrow, thus achieving greater accuracy downrange.

Stabilizers are rods of varying lengths that contain end weights to help stabilize the bow prior to and after the release of the arrow. They also absorb some of the shock, or recoil, that a bow naturally has. Stabilizers can be used singly in the front of the bow, or as part of a balancing

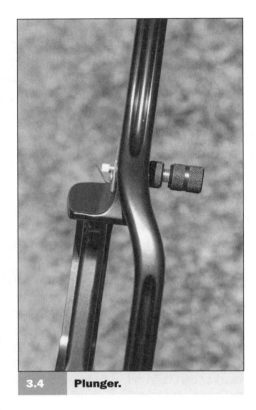

3.4 **Plunger.**

system using a single rod (sometimes called a side rod) or two rods referred to as v-bars. A front stabilizer is screwed into a threaded hole on the front of the bow, below the grip. When stabilized properly, a bow is steadier in the wind (and overall) and falls forward slightly as the arrow is released. Stabilizers are often chosen according to the preference of the archer and the coach, and are highly customized in terms of length and weight. They vary in terms of vibration dampening, weight, material, and length. When selecting a stabilizer, always consult the manufacturer, an archery retailer, or a certified coach to determine the proper length and weight for you.

CLICKERS

Clickers were first invented by archers who wanted to know when they had pulled the bowstring back to a certain point, to improve their consistency. A clicker, commonly used on recurve bows, is a strip of metal or carbon that is screwed into the bow riser and hangs downward toward the shelf. The arrow is positioned between the clicker and the riser. When pulled back, the point of the arrow eventually slides past the clicker as the archer completes the *aiming and expansion* step of shooting, which causes the clicker to hit the riser with a slight clicking sound. This sound, and the slight vibration you may feel when it clicks, tells you that you have pulled the bowstring back the proper distance for consistent arrow speed, and that it's time to take the shot.

You will need to adjust your clicker using the arrows you will use in competition. Be sure to work with a certified archer or coach when setting up your clicker for the first time. If the clicker is too far back or too far forward, it can cause injury; moreover, both issues create poor habits that can later be difficult to correct. With practice, experienced archers often report that they no longer hear the click, but instead they sense it as part of their overall mental game. Clickers are generally found only on recurve bows because compound bows have a draw stop built into them.

SLINGS AND CHEST PROTECTORS

Because archers are taught to hold the bow with little effort, there's a risk the bow will fly out of their hands upon release of the bowstring. Slings were created to catch the bow. They tend to relax archers because they are no longer anxious about dropping the bow upon release. Wrist slings are common with compound bows; some recurve archers also favor wrist slings, and many use finger slings (figure 3.5). You can purchase a commercial sling, or you can use wide,

3.5   **Finger sling.**

flat shoelaces to tie a finger sling that is not only practical, but also fun to look at. Like finger tabs, slings are among the most-often-lost accessories on an archery field, so be sure to have a backup.

Archers are often taught to wear fitted clothing when shooting so as not to snag the bowstring upon release. However, recurve archers still commonly wear chest protectors just to make sure this doesn't happen. A chest protector also helps prevent chest contact with the bowstring for both men and women. It is slipped over the shoulder opposite the draw hand and fastened with adjustable straps. Chest protectors come in lots of materials and colors; choose one that is tight fitting but not uncomfortable. It is meant to fit close to the body so that the string slides smoothly off it if there is any contact.

COMPOUND BOW ACCESSORIES

Compound bows use accessories that aren't used with recurve bows—particularly, the peep sight and mechanical release aid. A peep sight is a small ring tied into the bowstring through which you look while lining up the sight with the distant target—essentially lining up the target in the sight, and the sight in the peep sight. The peep sight, sometimes called a rear sight, is intended to line up perfectly with your eye when the bow is at full draw. A peep sight is not easily adjustable after being installed, so it's critical to get its position accurate on the bowstring. First invented for use in bowhunting, peep sights are generally allowed on compound bows in competitions. (Chapter 7 includes information on using peep sights.)

Another accessory for compound bows is the mechanical release aid, a small, hinged clip that fastens onto the bowstring near the arrow nock and triggers the release of the bowstring. When it's activated by squeezing or some other method once you are at full draw, the clip releases the bowstring. Mechanical releases offer a more accurate release than the fingers do by preventing any side-to-side twisting of the bowstring. Mechanical releases vary in how they are activated, how many fingers they accommodate, size, color, and whether they have a safety or not. (Use of the mechanical release is covered in chapter 5.)

Equipment Setups

In archery each setup is unique and suited to a particular type of competition. Four commonly used setups are traditional, target, field, and 3D.

Traditional archers use the bare minimum of equipment (figure 3.6). The traditional archer prefers to shoot barebow because it lacks any sights or accessories. This type of archer shoots the arrow right off the shelf of the bow with the fingers. Some traditional archers shoot with a regular finger tab like other archers; others wear a special glove that protects the three drawing fingers but leaves the inside of the hand open. This glove is often used by traditional archers who shoot using all-wood bows and all-wood arrows. An arm guard is also a necessity for the traditional archer. The bow may be a simple straight longbow or a wooden recurve. The quiver is slung over the back or hung at the side, and the handmade arrows might sport real feathers in a variety of colors. Traditional archers may use wood, aluminum, or carbon arrows, which are sometimes crested to give a more authentic look and feel to the arrow shaft.

Do you have Olympic or Paralympic dreams? Archers focused on Olympic-style target archery use all the latest accessories on highly engineered recurve bows (figure 3.7). Their recurve bows are manufactured with a variety of composites and are finely tuned for accuracy. They spend many hours adjusting and tuning their bows and arrows for perfect fit and function. The bows are steadied by stabilizers and side rod setups, and high-performance arrow rests and precision sights are go-to accessories. The side quiver contains a finger tab, a finger sling, an arm guard (when it isn't being worn), a towel, an arrow puller (a split rubber tube used for getting a better grip on an arrow being pulled from the target), arrow lubricant,

3.6 Traditional (barebow) archery setup using a longbow.

Olympic-style archery setup using a recurve bow.

and other accessories introduced by fellow archers and by attending tournaments. Compound archers—who shoot target archery—sport many similar equipment options, but these are adapted to the compound bow. These archers wear form-fitting clothing on their upper bodies as well as chest protectors (for recurve archers), and their hair is up and out of their eyes. They may sport sunglasses or hats or visors to cut down on glare. They might also have a spotting scope on a stand so they can see their arrows on distant targets better and adjust their sights accordingly. A pen and pencil, along with a small notepad, are a must for every competitive archer.

Compound archers who enjoy 3D, field, or target archery set up a fast compound bow with an arrow rest, sight, stabilizer, and often a side rod (figure 3.8). This type of bow setup might also include specially designed shock absorbers either built into the bow or fastened to the limbs. The side quiver also contains a wrench set to make any last-minute repairs or adjustments. Because this archer moves from shooting station to shooting station, a spotting scope is generally not necessary—but binoculars are a must. The bow has an adjustable arrow rest and a precision sight, and that sight has a

3.8 Field or 3D archery setup using a compound bow.

magnified lens, or scope, along with a level for making sure the bow is straight when shooting. In addition to the side quiver, this archer wears a pouch on the belt to hold a release aid; in the quiver are a towel, arrow puller, arrow lubricant, and of course a small notepad, as well as a pen and pencil.

On Target

Archery accessories can greatly increase your accuracy and enjoyment of the sport. Be sure, however, to choose accessories to match your style of archery, and resist the temptation to purchase them until you have established a consistent shooting form. Get your instructor or coach, and your local archery retailer, to help you choose accessories that bring out your best.

Shooting Recurve

Archery is a sport that requires consistency in form, despite variables in your equipment, the environment, and other shooting conditions. To shoot tight groups (i.e., clusters of arrows in your target), or even just to hit what you're aiming at, you have to be able to identify these variables and embrace the secret to archery success: consistency. If you are a fan of archery and watch archers shooting in the Olympic or Paralympic Games or the World Championships, you'll notice that all of the archers are very, very good, yet few of them use exactly the same technique to shoot the arrow. This is because the best archers in the world are usually the most consistent archers in the world—even if they sometimes use unique shooting techniques.

That said, there are shooting techniques that set a foundation of consistency from the beginning. This chapter takes you through a proven method to learn how to shoot a bow accurately even if you've never held a bow before. As exciting as that prospect may be, remember at all times to make safety your primary concern.

Stringing Your Recurve Bow

Stringing your bow properly can save wear on the limbs by limiting torque, or stress. If the bow is strung incorrectly, at minimum the limbs may be irreparably damaged, and at worst, the limbs may suddenly flip out of control and strike your face or eyes. Take care and pay close attention while stringing your bow. Although the stringing process is described in this chapter, it's important to get an in-person demonstration on stringing your bow from your local archery store or coach.

To begin, put the bowstring on the bow by securing it to the limbs. At this point, because the bow is unstrung, the string will have considerable slack in it. Bowstrings generally come with two different-sized loops at the ends. Slide the larger string loop over the upper bow limb, and the smaller loop over the tip and into the string groove of the lower bow limb. Secure the lower loop into the string groove with a tightly wrapped rubber band, but first be certain that the string loop is correctly secured onto both sides of the limb tip.

Stringing your bow requires a simple but important accessory called a bowstringer. Manufacturers modify the design of this handy tool somewhat, but it generally functions in one of two ways. A bowstringer has either a cord with leather pockets tied onto both ends, or a single pocket on one end and a flat piece with a loop on the other. The double-pocket version is more suited to a longbow than a recurve bow, whereas the pocket-and-flat-piece variety is more appropriate for a recurve bow.

This explanation describes the steps a right-handed archer would follow to string a recurve bow using the pocket-and-flat piece type of bowstringer. If you are left-handed, simply reverse the hands used in each step.

To begin, cover the lower limb tip with the bowstringer pocket, ensuring that the string is secured on both sides of the limb tip prior to sliding the pocket into place (figure 4.1). Then, slide the flat piece of the bowstringer over the top limb of the bow, so that it rests a few inches (around 8 cm) below the limb tip and—this is very important—behind the top loop of the bowstring (figure 4.2). You'll use that flat piece to stabilize and compress the top limb so that you can slide the bowstring up and into the grooves on the limb tip. Turn the bow so that it is horizontal and the limbs are facing up toward the sky. At this point, the slack in the bowstringer will be low, touching the ground, the bowstringer pocket will be covering the lower limb tip, and the flat part of the bowstringer will be just behind the bowstring

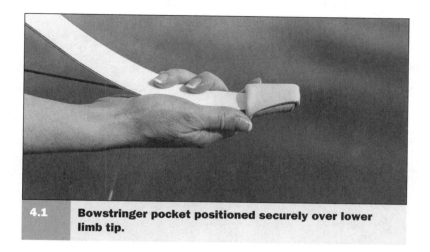

4.1 Bowstringer pocket positioned securely over lower limb tip.

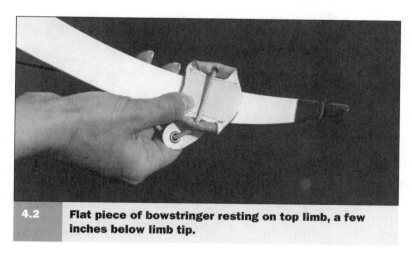

4.2 Flat piece of bowstringer resting on top limb, a few inches below limb tip.

loop on the top limb. Be sure there is enough slack in the bowstringer cord so that you can safely step on it and that there are no tangles in the bowstring itself.

Next, hold the bow by the grip with your left hand, and steady the large bowstring loop against the upper bow limb with your other hand. Step on the bowstringer cord with both feet planted at least shoulder-width apart for stability. Begin to pull up on the bow with your left hand; this essentially draws the bow using the bowstringer, and the limbs compress, allowing you to secure the string.

How do you secure the string? As you are pulling up on the bow, take your right hand and slide the top bowstring loop along the limb until it is in place on both sides of the limb tip (figure 4.3). Be absolutely certain the bowstring is completely secured on the limb tip, and then *slowly* begin to bring the bow down toward the stringer

Position the bowstring loop in the grooves.

cord with your left hand. If the string is not fully secured on either end of the bow, it will slip off the limb and the limb will move—very quickly—in the direction of your face.

Once the bowstring is securely on both sides of the upper limb tip, and you've slowly let down tension, immediately turn the bow away from you and do a safety check to see that the string is secured completely on both limbs (figure 4.4). This way, if an accident should occur, the limbs will move in a direction other than directly toward you.

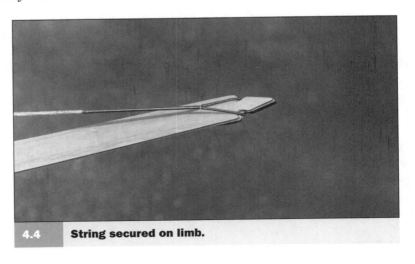

4.4 **String secured on limb.**

If you see that the string is not fully secured, immediately put the bowstringer back on, but keep the limbs facing away from you and other people. Point the bow in the direction of your target, if possible. Quickly turn the bow over and repeat the stringing process, but be sure not to look directly over the limb—keep your head away from the limb with the unsecured string until the string is completely secured. Redo your safety check, and you're good to go!

Unstringing the bow is very much the same process, except in reverse. Put the lower pocket on the fully strung lower limb tip, and the flat piece against the upper part of the top limb, where the limb begins to curve out. Holding the bow with your left hand (if you are right-handed), pull up on the bow so that the stringer draws the bow, creating slack in the bowstring. Reach to the upper limb and slip the string over the limb tip, sliding the bowstring loop down over the limb. Gently let down the tension on the bow by slowly bringing the bow back toward the ground.

It is generally okay to leave your bow strung during a day of shooting. However, to relieve the strain on the bow limbs, unstring the bow when you will not be using it for an extended period.

More to choose and use

PUTTING ON A FINGER TAB
AND ARM GUARD

Finger tabs and arm guards are a must anytime you're shooting a recurve bow. They are intended to protect the fingers of your draw hand, and the inside of your bow arm (the side holding the bow), from blisters and abrasions, respectively. Use them from the beginning of your training, and encourage others to use them as well. The arm guard is positioned on your bow arm to protect the inside of your arm below the elbow. Arm guards are generally made of leather, plastic, or reinforced cloth and may have a plastic strip in the middle. Fasten the arm guard and adjust the tightness of the straps if necessary (figure 4.5). It should fit snugly without twisting. In general, it should be midway between your wrist and elbow. If you find that you are hurting the inside of your arm despite the presence of an arm guard, you may have a form-related issue or be double-jointed. If either is the case, as a beginner, you may want to try a full-length arm guard, which has a lower and an upper part and creases at the elbow. This provides additional protection and support while you learn proper shooting technique. The arm guard is placed on the inside of your

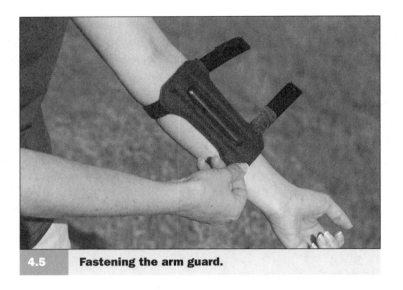

Fastening the arm guard.

bow arm (i.e., the left arm if you are right-handed; the right arm if you are left-handed).

Finger tabs are generally made from soft leather and may have a single or double layer to protect the fingertips from the abrasion of the bowstring. To put one on, hold the tab in your bow hand and place the middle finger of your draw hand into the hole on the finger tab. Slide the tab down your finger until the separator (if included) rests between your index and middle fingers and the leather or backing rests against the inside of your fingers (figure 4.6). The finger tab is worn on the draw hand (i.e., the right hand if you are right-handed; the left hand if you are left-handed).

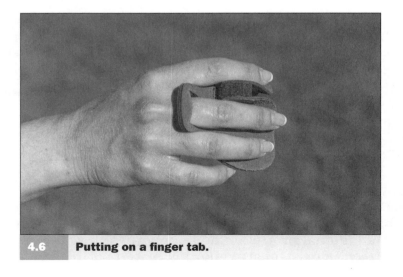

4.6 **Putting on a finger tab.**

Shooting a Recurve Bow

You can actually practice some shooting steps without using a bow. Raising your bow arm up and down while keeping your shoulders down and relaxed and pretending to draw your bow back until your forefinger reaches the corner of your smile while standing straight and tall—all of this builds muscle memory.

When you are learning to shoot your first arrows, you don't even need a target face (the paper target that is affixed to the foam target mat or bag-style target). Just shoot at a blank target, mat, or bag. The target should be as close to you as possible without interfering with your form—as close as 5 to 10 yards to start. At this point, all you're doing is learning the correct form and shooting sequence.

The following shooting technique, derived from steps developed by the USA Archery national head coach, KiSik Lee, is a good primer to help you get started. As always, it's best to receive proper instruction from a certified instructor or coach, or a licensed USA Archery club. However, for the purposes of getting started on your own, the steps presented in the following list are a great way to begin. In addition, remember to follow the standard range whistle commands—two blasts signal that you should go to the shooting line, one blast signals that it's safe to shoot, and three blasts signal that it's time to retrieve your arrows. If you ever hear four or more whistle blasts, that signals *stop shooting immediately*. This means there's an emergency on the archery range.

Recurve Shooting: Getting Started

The key concepts in shooting a recurve bow, adapted from USA Archery's *Archery*, are as follows:

1. Stance
2. Nocking the arrow
3. Hooking the string and gripping the bow
4. Set position and mind-set
5. Setup
6. Drawing and loading
7. Anchoring
8. Transferring and holding
9. Aiming and expansion
10. Releasing and following through

This may seem like a complex set of steps, but actually, this step-by-step process for shooting a bow is quite simple and provides a great foundation for proper shooting technique. It is explained here in a way that should make sense to beginners.

1. *Stance.* Your stance is your connection to the ground; it gives you stability while making the shot. Start by standing perpendicular to the target. If you're a right-handed archer, this means you are holding the bow in your left hand and will eventually draw the string with your right hand. Your shoulders should be parallel to the target. Place one foot on either side of the shooting line, approximately shoulder-width apart. Ensure that your weight is approximately 60 percent on the front of your feet and 40 percent on your heels, to avoid rocking backward during the shot. At this point, shift into an open stance. Move your bow-side foot back so that the toe of the bow-side foot lines up to the ball of the draw-side foot. Now, turn about 25 degrees toward your target (figure 4.7). Your hips should be in line with your feet.

4.7   Stance.

2. Nocking the arrow. Pull an arrow from your quiver, holding it by its nock. Place the arrow on the arrow rest of your bow, and position the arrow so the index vane (the odd-colored one) faces you and is perpendicular to the bowstring. Fit the nock onto the string directly below your nock locator. You should hear and feel the nock snap into place on the string (figure 4.8). Remember, if you see a crack or break in the nock, put that arrow aside for repair and select another arrow to shoot.

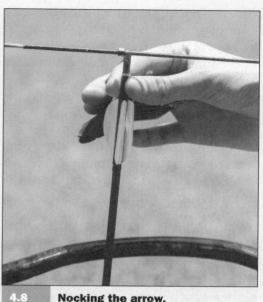

4.8 **Nocking the arrow.**

3. Hooking the string and gripping the bow. Two of the most important parts of the shot are hooking the bowstring and gripping the bow (figure 4.9, *a* and *b*). These are both points of physical

4.9 **(a) Hooking the string and (b) gripping the bow.**

contact with the bow, and doing these steps consistently will go a long way toward achieving good groups in your target. First, place the fingers of your draw hand on the bowstring, with the string running across what is often called the archer's groove (just before the first groove on the index finger, just behind the groove on the middle finger, and just in front of the groove on the ring finger). Your thumb and pinkie finger should be tucked beneath your draw hand, the back of your hand should be flat and relaxed, and your wrist should be in a relaxed, natural position—even slightly out. Never invert your wrist toward your body because this can cause injury.

Next, place your bow hand on the grip of the bow. With the palm of your hand facing your target, place the V between your thumb and forefinger in the grip of the bow. Lower the meaty part of your thumb onto the middle of the bow grip, so that you apply pressure to the middle of the bow grip from the base of your thumb, just to the right of the lifeline on your palm (if you are right-handed). Your thumb should point toward the target, your index finger can rest gently on the front of the bow, and your remaining fingers should be curled under themselves, which naturally brings the knuckles of your hand back toward you.

4. Set position and mind-set. This is a great time to double-check your stance, hook, and grip, and to make sure everything is in the right position. Take a deep breath through your belly, and as you release that breath, keep your head up but relax your shoulders, so that you are standing straight with your shoulders relaxed. Keep your back flat and your hips in line with your feet. Finally, look directly at the target (figure 4.10). Be sure that you maintain your posture as you begin the rest of the shot sequence. Now is a great time to tell yourself what you're going to concentrate on for this particular shot.

5. Setup. Slowly raise the bow, keeping a bit of tension on the bowstring with your draw hand, so that the bow is partially drawn as it is raised. Raise the bow by letting your arms move up in a hinging motion, so that both the bow hand and the draw hand come up together as the shoulders stay low and relaxed. Keep your draw elbow just above the height of your draw hand. Raise your bow arm until it is approximately nose height and your draw hand to approximately mouth height. If there is a sight on your bow, just allow the aperture to float around the target; it's not yet time to hold it steady or aim. As you raise the bow, you may turn slightly at the waist, keeping your hips still, so that your shoulders remain perpendicular to the target (figure 4.11).

4.10 Set position and mind-set.

4.11 Setup.

6. *Drawing and loading.* The goal in this step is to draw the bowstring back using the big, strong muscles in your back rather than the weaker muscles in your arm. Draw your bow back by rotating the draw-side elbow around the draw-side shoulder (figure 4.12). Think of pushing your draw-side shoulder blade (scapula) and the back of your draw arm in a semicircle around your body. Keep your draw hand relaxed and your shoulders low, and maintain a nice, straight posture. Continue this drawing motion throughout the rest of the shot, even when the movements of the shot become much smaller.

4.12　**Drawing and loading.**

7. *Anchoring.* Your anchor point is a point of stability—a point you consistently draw the bowstring back to that hopefully helps you to hit the same place on your target each time (figure 4.13). Having drawn the bowstring back so that the index finger of your draw hand comes straight to the corner of your mouth (the right side of your smile if you are right-handed) or under your jaw, make firm contact there as you continue to maintain tension in the back of your drawing arm and in your back, in the same direction you began in step 6, drawing and loading.

4.13　**Anchoring using under-the-jaw anchor point.**

8. *Transferring and holding.* This step begins with a small transfer of energy that you make by moving the back of your draw arm just a bit farther down the shooting line; this shifts most of the weight of the bow into the stronger muscles in your back. Think of the transfer as moving your draw-side elbow down the shooting line. This motion will help you achieve the best possible alignment with the bow, which is called holding (figure 4.14).

4.14 **Transferring and holding.**

9. *Aiming and expansion.* Aiming is the process of focusing your eyes and concentration on the center of your target. While you are aiming, keep your bowstring lined up with the center of your sight (for a corner-of-the-mouth anchor point), which functions as a rear sight for a recurve bow, and helps to control the tendency to group arrows to the left or right of center. Most important in aiming is that you not hold the aperture completely still on your target; rather, aim while you focus on maintaining the tension in your back that you established during step 8, transferring and holding. As you aim and maintain tension in your back for two to three seconds, you should feel a stretch from within your chest. This is called expansion (figure 4.15).

4.15 **Aiming and expansion.**

10. *Releasing and following through.* Now, it's time to release the arrow. To accomplish a good, clean release, simply allow the bow-string to push your fingers out of the way as you continue the motion you started earlier in step 6, drawing and loading. In other words, pull through the release, relaxing your draw-hand fingers completely as you release the bowstring, which will initiate the follow-through (figure 4.16). Keep your draw-side elbow moving back and around; if you maintain proper tension in your back, this motion will pull your draw-side elbow in the correct direction. The ideal is that your draw-hand fingers stay close to your cheek, and the motion of your draw-side elbow and the release of the bowstring pulls your hand back toward your ear. Follow-through should be a natural conse-quence of tension in the draw side of your back. Think of it as the motion that continues when a pro golfer hits the ball, or when a ten-nis player swings a racket or a baseball player swings a bat. These athletes don't simply stop short when they make a connection with the ball (or in your case, when you release the bowstring). Correct shooting technique will keep the draw elbow coming back and the back engaged, allowing you to finish the shot with strength.

Note: If you've watched archery, you may have noticed that the bow often appears to drop from the bow hand upon the release of the arrow. In fact, there is a specific technique for releasing the bow.

4.16   **Releasing and following through.**

However, this is considered an intermediate to advanced archery technique. If you want to learn this technique, check with your coach, and refer to the book *Archery* for more information on intermediate shooting techniques. As a beginning archer, you may or may not have a stabilizer on your bow yet that pulls the bow forward after the shot. The best technique to learn at this stage is to relax the thumb and forefinger of the bow hand as you release and follow through with the draw hand. However, be sure you're wearing a wrist or finger sling when you do so. Learning this relaxation technique at the beginning stages of shooting is far preferable to the alternative—training yourself to catch or grab the bow after the shot, which can be a difficult mistake to correct as you continue shooting.

Although not generally considered part of the actual shooting sequence, pulling and carrying your arrows properly is a point of safety and etiquette for archers. Approach your target from one side. Be sure to look behind you, and check that nobody is standing near the target. Standing to either the right or left side, place your outspread hand onto the target face and around the arrow. Grasp the arrow with your other hand as close to the target as possible, and gently pull the arrow straight out of the target. Rotate the arrow carefully if it sticks. Check behind you before pulling each arrow.

Once you have removed the arrow, place it into your side quiver and continue pulling arrows out of the target and placing them in your side quiver until you are finished. Walk back to the shooting line, and place the arrows into your ground quiver, if applicable. If you aren't wearing a side quiver, arrows should always be carried using both hands, horizontally, with one hand covering the points and the other hand holding the group of arrows firmly below the fletchings.

Give it a go

SHOOTING AT DIFFERENT TARGETS

Now that you have learned the basic recurve shooting technique, place a target face onto your mat and practice shooting while aiming at an actual target. It's only important at this point to get used to having an actual target in front of you. Focus on your form and the shooting sequence, and not necessarily on scoring. Take your time and establish a rhythm while shooting; a good tip is to count slowly to 10 between arrows to give your mind time to evaluate your last shot and refocus on the next. A handy tip is to have only three arrows in your quiver. There's a tendency to rush your shooting if you have a whole quiver full of arrows, so limit yourself to three.

You'd think it would be easier to hit a big target up close, but sometimes it's easier to hit a smaller one. Consider forgoing the standard 80- or 122-centimeter (31 or 48 in.) outdoor target faces at distances of less than 18 meters (20 yd), and instead try a 40- or 60-centimeter (16 or 24 in.) target face, or a balloon. With a small target, your eyes tend to focus in on a small target better than on a bigger one, and you're likely to pay more attention to your shooting form. A great small target to use is a balloon. Balloons are easy to use because they can be blown up to different sizes, they can be placed almost anywhere on the target mat, and they pop when you hit them. Archers of all ages love them! Balloons and other novelty targets are a great way to make archery enjoyable. They also help you learn how to judge distance, develop aiming skills, and have fun competitions with your friends.

Later in this book you'll learn some advanced shooting techniques and exercises. In the meantime, here are a few exercises to help you with the basics.

STAND STRAIGHT AND SHOOT STRAIGHT

Most problems in developing proper shooting form can be attributed to forgetting a basic rule—stand up straight and tall. But even though you are reminding yourself to stand erect, are you really doing it? Many archers think they are standing straight when in fact they are leaning back or forward or to one side or the other. This is often caused by using the wrong muscles to draw the bow, or allowing the posture to change during the shot process.

To really determine how straight you are standing, ask your instructor or a shooting partner to observe you or take some photos or a video of your shot mechanics. Your head and body should be straight, your shoulders low and relaxed, and the elbow of your drawing arm just above level. Remember, shooting incorrectly when you start will form poor habits quickly that can be difficult to unlearn. Instead, be sure you're taking your time and taking each shot step-by-step to ensure long-term archery success.

BUCKET DROP

Proper string release is vital to becoming an accurate archer. Here's a simple exercise to learn how to release a string smoothly while keeping the back of your hand relaxed. Fill a bucket with water or sand until it weighs about 10 pounds (4.5 kg). With your draw hand, and using your finger tab, lift the bucket by the handle a few inches (about 8 cm) off the ground, using the same muscles you use to draw the bow (figure 4.17a). Keep the back of your hand relaxed and your wrist in the proper position for shooting a bow. Now release the bucket and let it fall, following through with your back (figure 4.17b). Notice how the bucket handle just slips through your fingers. Do this exercise several dozen times until it becomes instinctive. Then resume shooting your bow (figure 4.17c). Notice how much smoother your release is and how little effort it now takes to let go of the bowstring at full draw.

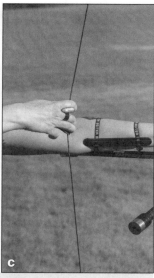

4.17 Bucket drop involves (a) lifting the bucket by the handle, (b) releasing the bucket and following through, and (c) using the same technique with your bow.

On Target

Following a consistent routine is the key to becoming a great archer. If you are new to archery, just concentrate on developing proper shooting form. Don't worry right now about accuracy or even how far away the target is. Focus only on the arrow that's on the string, and repeat each step, one at a time, until you gain confidence with your shooting technique.

Shooting Compound

Unlike a recurve bow, a compound bow is made up of a unique system of limbs, cables, wheels, and cams. Energy is stored in the bow when it is drawn back, as with a recurve. However, because of the inclusion of one or more cams, the holding draw weight is drastically reduced at full draw (an action called let-off). This reduction in draw weight allows the archer to hold the bow at full draw at a fraction of the peak draw weight. This is incredibly useful in bowhunting and in competitive archery, when compound archers are holding the bow back much longer than recurve archers do, while aiming.

Because of the cams, the compound bow comes to a complete stop at full draw, which means that the bow must be properly fitted to the archer in terms of draw length. Achieving individual fit is critical, and this must be done by a professional at an archery retailer. Some compound bows are very specifically fitted to the archer, meaning that they are built for a specific draw length and cannot be adjusted. Other compound bows can be adjusted to accommodate a range of draw lengths. On the other hand, most compound bows can be adjusted to draw weight, usually within a range of 10 pounds (4.5 kg). Once the bow has been matched to your draw length and draw weight, you can use it safely because its designed functions now work in concert with your body movements.

Holding and Using Your Compound Bow

Once you've had your compound bow adjusted for your unique size, you can begin shooting it and gaining experience. In the early years of the compound bow, many archers shot this bow with their fingers, using recurve style, but the majority of compound archers now favor the use of a mechanical release aid. Indeed, most currently manufactured compound bows are designed to be shot this way. Although it may look radically different from a recurve bow, the compound has similar design features (figure 5.1). It has upper and lower limbs, a riser with a sight window, a handle with a grip, and standard-sized holes with threaded metal inserts to accept a number of accessories.

You hold a compound bow similarly to the way you hold a recurve. The grip may be molded or attached to the handle, and some compound bows also offer the option of no extra grip at all—the machined handle of the bow serves as the grip. You may wonder how a bow can function without a shaped grip, and it's actually quite simple: Compound bows are sensitive to torque—in this case, the pressure from your hand that affects the flight of the arrow and the outcome of the shot. When your hand rests just on the machined handle of

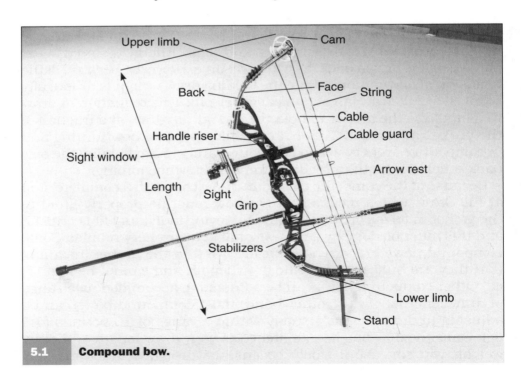

5.1   **Compound bow.**

the bow (which some archers cover with grip tape for stability), the proper pressure point is more accurately placed on the bow, lessening torque.

Whatever the grip option on your compound bow, your hand will rest comfortably in it as the bow becomes a natural extension of your arm. You may notice that a compound bow can be a bit heavier than a recurve bow, and you may tend to lean back to provide leverage. To compensate for the heavier weight of the bow, many archers ensure that bow weight feels balanced with draw weight, and shoot with an open stance, as with the recurve bow (figure 5.2). In other words, the weight that one side of your body is holding up is counterbalanced by the weight the other side of your body is drawing back and then holding. The open stance gives your body better balance while standing up straight and helps you maintain proper form.

Adjustable, user-friendly models without a let-off are available for young people or those who are just starting out in the sport. These are not true compound bows, in a sense, because they draw more like recurves. This type of bow is popular among recreation program directors because one bow can fit the body size and draw length of most archers.

For archers who are beginning in the sport, a bow with a greater range of draw length and weight adjustment is often desired, because shooting form tends to change a bit with gains in strength and experience. If you are just beginning to explore archery and do not know whether you want to hunt, target shoot, enjoy 3D or field archery, or shoot recreationally, you would do well to purchase a more adjustable model.

If you want to make more of a long-term investment in archery equipment and know what you want, countless compound bows are available at most archery retailers. You can find a variety of bows specifically designed for the type of archery you're planning to enjoy, with characteristics that contribute to speed, a smooth draw, and other attributes to enhance your shooting experience.

Mechanical releases are popular with compound archers because they allow them to hold and release the string more steadily than they can with their fingers. Also, compound

5.2 Using an open stance to shoot a compound bow.

bows are far shorter than recurves, which means that the string angle is sharper at full draw. The disadvantage to pulling a compound bowstring back with the fingers is that it may cause the fingers to become pinched around the arrow nock, causing the nock to pop off the string or the arrow to keep falling off the arrow rest. That said, there are still competition classes for finger shooters with compounds, and they generally use bows that are longer axle to axle for a smoother draw and more forgiving string angle. In general, though, a mechanical release aid produces the best and most consistent results.

More to choose and use

MECHANICAL RELEASES

Several standard forms of mechanical releases are available. All use some form of trigger device that releases the string (figure 5.3). Many releases use the thumb or finger to activate the trigger, and other releases use a safety until the archer reaches full draw and then become activated when additional back tension is used. Mechanical releases work based on the fact that the compound bow draws back only a specified distance and then stops—unlike a recurve bow that you can continue to pull back and that has no specific draw length.

Releases can clip directly onto the string serving between the two nock locators that are commonly found on compound bows. They can

5.3   **Mechanical release hooked onto bowstring.**

also be clipped to a loop of material called a D-loop that surrounds the nock and pulls the string back evenly. Always keep safety concerns in mind when using a mechanical release. Make sure the bow is pointed in a safe direction, and be very aware of the design features of your release. Releases are designed to activate suddenly with very little effort. The goal is a surprise upon releasing the bowstring. Avoid becoming startled or distracted during the shot, because the release aid can activate unexpectedly.

ADJUSTING DRAW WEIGHT

The draw weight of most compound bows can be adjusted easily. Changing the draw weight generally does not affect the draw length; however, it does affect the tune of the bow—that is, how much the arrows flex in flight, which can affect how the arrows group in the target. Generally, you should adjust the draw weight of your bow with the assistance of your instructor, your coach, or an archery retailer.

The lower limb usually has a manufacturer's decal that indicates the peak draw weight of that particular bow. Each limb may have a bolt that holds it in the limb pocket. This limb bolt can be turned with a wrench. By loosening the bolt (turning it counterclockwise) a given number of turns, you decrease the draw weight by a specific amount as defined by the manufacturer's instructions. Likewise, the draw weight can be increased by turning the limb bolts clockwise. Both limbs should be equal, so be sure to either tighten or loosen them the same number of turns. The manufacturer's instructions may indicate how many turns of the nut equals how much of a reduction in draw weight. The instructions may also state the minimum weight that is safe for that bow to still function. If the limbs are loosened beyond that safe range, serious damage to the bow may result. For this reason, it is a good idea to meet with the retailer who sold you the bow prior to making these adjustments.

ADJUSTING DRAW LENGTH

Adjusting draw length on most compound bows requires a special tool to hold the bow and also compress it safely to release the string and cables. Archery coaches and retailers use this tool, called a bow press, to help archers adjust their compound bows. On some bows, draw length can be adjusted by moving a module along the edge of a cam. This adjustment changes the length of the string at full draw, and it maintains the bow's draw weight let-off at that new distance. Once the string has been reinstalled, the bow is safely released from the bow press. The archery retailer or coach carefully inspects the bow to be sure it's safe to shoot again, and the archer tests it for proper draw length fit. Draw length should be double-checked by your archery coach or local archery retailer prior to shooting the bow.

ADJUSTING CENTER SHOT

To adjust center shot, nock an arrow onto the bowstring, and look down the shaft of the arrow. You should see the nock of the arrow attached to the bowstring and the bowstring superimposed over the limbs of the bow. The bowstring itself will appear to bisect the limbs of the bow. This is the case for both compound and recurve bows. On a recurve bow, for a right-handed archer, the point of the arrow is often slightly outside the bowstring alignment to the left (figure 5.4). On compound bows, the point of the arrow is often in line with the bowstring alignment. However, for both types of bows, the correct center shot will depend on several variables and can be individual to the archer and bow setup.

5.4   **Adjusting center shot.**

Take it to the range

Shooting a Compound Bow

Unlike a recurve bow, a compound bow is usually (but not always) shot with a mechanical release, which does not roll the string left to right. Compound bows therefore are generally not outfitted with a plunger. To position center shot properly, the arrow rest itself is often designed to adjust side to side. The adjustment can be seen plainly in the shifting position of the arrow point. To adjust and fine-tune your bow, your coach or retailer may use a piece of paper clipped to a frame; this is referred to as paper-tuning your bow. The coach or retailer shoots an arrow and looks for a bullet hole tear in the paper—one that does not show the arrow tearing left, right, up, or down. Any of these aberrations from a bullet hole tear indicates that an adjustment is needed; however, simply adjusting the arrow rest often takes care of the problem.

The steps presented in the following list and the instructions are addressed to an archer using a compound bow with a mechanical release aid that connects to the serving using a D-loop, a rear peep sight (a small circle installed in the bowstring), and a sight on the bow.

Compound Shooting: Getting Started

The steps of shooting a compound bow, adapted from USA Archery's *Archery*, are as follows:

1. Stance
2. Nocking the arrow
3. Hooking the string and gripping the bow
4. Setup and drawing
5. Anchoring
6. Transferring and holding
7. Aiming and expansion
8. Releasing and following through

1. Stance. Place one foot on either side of the shooting line. To achieve better string clearance and maximum stability, choose an open stance. With your weight distributed equally between your feet, feet shoulder-width apart, and about 60 percent of your weight on the front of your feet, rotate in place so that your feet and hips are open at approximately a 25- or 30-degree angle to the target (figure 5.5). The toe of your bow-side foot (front foot) should be in line with the ball of your draw-side foot. (For a square, or straight, stance, the weight distribution is the same, but you stand perpendicular to the target while shooting.) Be sure your back is flat, your head is up straight, and your shoulders are low and relaxed. Address the target.

5.5　Stance.

2. *Nocking the arrow.* Place the arrow onto the arrow rest, and nock the arrow onto the bowstring between the nocking points (figure 5.6). You will need to check with your coach, local archery retailer, or manufacturer's instructions regarding appropriate placement of your arrows on your arrow rest, so that the fletchings clear the rest when you release the arrow from the bow. Open your mechanical release and clip it onto the D-loop, ensuring that the release aid jaw is locked securely onto the loop.

| 5.6 | Nocking the arrow. |

3. *Hooking the string and gripping the bow.* Start by positioning your draw hand on the release aid in the appropriate position for the release you have. Be sure your fingers are well clear of the trigger so that when you draw the bow, there is no early release that could lead to serious injury. Next, position your hand on the grip of the bow; the meaty part of your thumb should form a pressure point on the middle of the grip. Every person's pressure point placement is unique, so be sure to experiment with this to see what gives you the best results. Your thumb should point toward the target, while your first finger rests lightly on the front of the grip. The remaining fingers curl back toward your palm, pulling the knuckles back toward you (figure 5.7, *a* and *b*).

| 5.7 | *(a)* Hooking the string and *(b)* gripping the bow. |

4. *Setup and drawing.* Begin putting some tension on the bowstring by drawing just a little as you raise your bow arm in a hinging motion, keeping your shoulders low. Be sure to keep the elbow of your draw arm at or just above the height of your draw-side wrist; in other words, do not lower your elbow to draw the bow. Draw the bowstring back firmly and smoothly (figure 5.8) through to the draw stop by rotating your draw-side

5.8 Setup and drawing.

elbow and using your back muscles. Maintain backward pressure on the bow while maintaining forward pressure on your bow arm, keeping your shoulders low and relaxed at all times.

5. *Anchoring.* Settle the bow into shooting position, and anchor your draw hand in the correct place along or under your jaw, depending on the type of release aid you're using (figure 5.9). If the bow is set up correctly, the bowstring should come into contact with your nose (at the same spot every time) as your hand connects with your jaw. This gives you two points of reference when anchoring. Your bone-on-bone alignment (further discussed in chapter 6) should take the bulk of the let-off draw weight.

5.9 Anchoring.

6. *Transferring and holding.* At this stage of the shot, you're literally transferring the last of the draw weight into your back. Although the compound bow lets off, it's crucial to keep tension in your back muscles and keep the back of your draw arm pointed down the shooting line behind you. When you reach natural alignment with the bow, you have reached holding, which is literally a state of alignment (figure 5.10). Holding does not mean stopping; it means keeping tension in your back muscles and keeping your draw arm moving in the same direction. As you feel settled in, rest your finger or thumb lightly on the trigger, depending on how your release aid is activated.

7. *Aiming and expansion.* Once you have transferred and reached holding, it's time to begin aiming. Look through the peep sight and line it up with your aperture or scope, which is essentially

5.10 **Transferring and holding.**

lining up the rear sight with the front sight. Allow your front sight to float over the target, and resist the urge to overaim; your brain will instinctively center your sight. Keep your bow level. Begin to feel an expansion from the center of your chest through to your back muscles as you maintain tension (figure 5.11).

5.11 **Aiming and expansion.**

8. *Releasing and following through.* Depending on the type of release you're using, as you continue to pull with your back muscles, the trigger of your release should be activated, releasing the bowstring and arrow. Your release aid may be triggered using your thumb, your forefinger, or just the tension in your hand, but triggering the release is not a deliberate act. Rather, your back tension sets off a chain reaction that pulls your draw elbow, your forearm, your wrist, and the part of your hand that activates the trigger. As the arrow leaves the bow, continue to extend your bow arm to the target until the arrow hits, as the draw arm follows through in a natural motion, pulled backward by the act of releasing tension in the bow. Maintain your focus on the target as you follow through, and keep your bow hand relaxed (figure 5.12). Your rear hand should remain relaxed until it comes to rest.

5.12 **Releasing and following through.**

COMPOUND BOW RELEASE AID

Practice aids are available to help you overcome any tendency to squeeze a mechanical release deliberately or suddenly (which throws your rear hand and body out of proper alignment). The use of such aids should be undertaken with the supervision of a trained compound bow coach or archery expert. Some release aid manufacturers sell releases that clip onto the bowstring normally but do not open when they are activated by the finger or by back tension. This type of device allows you to practice the steps of the compound bow shooting sequence without actually firing the bow. Practicing with a release aid will familiarize you with the feel of the mechanical release and how to activate it without additional hand motion.

You can easily make a simple aid, known as a cord loop, to practice proper release and follow-through technique. Tie a strong but thin cord into a loop that is nearly the length of your draw length and similar in diameter to your D-loop.

Have a partner, preferably a coach or retailer, spot you from behind when you use the cord loop. Hold the loop in your bow hand as you would the grip of your bow. Hook the other end of the loop with your mechanical release (figure 5.13). The length of the taut loop should be about 1 inch (2.5 cm) short of your full draw length.

5.13   **Use a cord loop to practice releasing and following through.**

To use the loop, attach your release and bring the loop to full draw. You can set your release against the tension of the loop. Using proper back motion, activate your release just as you would if it were attached to a real bow. The loose cord loop will spring forward from the release aid toward your bow hand, which is holding the front of the loop. This is a great training aid for practicing proper follow-through as well, because the loop won't spring forward if you are prone to resisting your natural follow-through.

On Target

Although the compound bow functions in a way that is radically different from a recurve, it's fun to shoot and offers exciting alternatives in accessories and technology. Always be sure to modify the settings of your bow to fit your draw length and draw weight, with the assistance of an archery coach or a knowledgeable expert. Compound bows are set up for individual archers, so do not share your compound bow with another archer.

The technology of compound bows has allowed archers and manufacturers to design and produce a wide variety of accessories. Take time in selecting your equipment and talk with knowledgeable archers and experts at pro shops about your choice of shooting styles. Be sure that your equipment can be used in your chosen archery activity legally and safely.

Alignment, Anchor Points, and Releases

Now that you know the basics of recurve and compound shooting form, it's time to fine-tune your technique. Keep in mind that everything you do at the shooting line affects your outcomes at the target. Also keep in mind that bodies are unique. As a result, not all techniques work the same for all archers. What's important is that your shooting technique be repeatable, shot after shot. Regardless of subtle differences, shooting techniques that rely on bone structure and biomechanics are more repeatable, because they make use of the strongest muscle groups in the body and are easiest for the muscles to learn.

Body Alignment

Think of your body as a solid and stable platform for the main points of contact with the bow: your hands. Remember that although your hands actually touch the bow, the string, and the arrow, your bones, muscles, and overall body structure must work together to create a repeatable shot. Before we discuss the hands, let's make sure your body is as stable as it can be.

Proper body alignment begins with your stance. Archers are usually required to straddle the shooting line, but the alignment of the feet is a matter of personal preference. To find your most stable stance, place your feet shoulder-width apart, with equal weight on both feet (figure 6.1). From this position you can experiment to find a stance that suits your body type and is comfortable; a coach can make some helpful suggestions as well.

Two popular options for the stance are an open stance and a square stance. In an open stance, the foot closer to the target is slightly behind the foot farther from the target, and the feet and hips are angled slightly toward the target (figure 6.2). In a square stance, the feet and hips are perpendicular to the target (figure 6.3). Whether shooting a compound or recurve bow, many archers find that an open stance keeps them more stable in the wind. Even top archers typically have some degree of openness in their stance.

Bone on bone is a phrase you might hear from an archery coach; it refers to aligning the bone structure found through the shoulders, into the wrist of the hand that grips the bow. Pulling back a bow requires muscle effort, but ideally, you draw the bow in a way that works with the biomechanics of your body. Your bones support the drawn bow so that your muscles can do the work of shooting the arrow. The way you set up the shot and draw the bow determines whether you are using

6.1 Balanced position.

6.2   Open stance.

6.3   Square stance.

your bone structure or relying on smaller and weaker muscles. Generally, keeping your shoulders even, your back flat, your stance balanced and comfortable, and your draw elbow inside the arrow line will result in a measure of bone-on-bone alignment (figure 6.4). Now that we've created a steady platform, let's look at the hands.

6.4   Bone-on-bone alignment.

GRIP

The most important thing to remember about the grip is to find and apply the correct pressure point. If you're a right-handed archer, this is found just to the right of the lifeline on your palm, at the meaty part of the base of the thumb, facing the back of your hand. To set grip position, place the area between the thumb and index finger into the thinnest part of the bow grip. Bring the pressure point down to the center of the grip, with the lifeline running down the left side of the bow.

Bow handles often have a grip, either molded in or attached, that is set at an average angle for most hands (figure 6.5). Some bow and after-market grip manufacturers offer specialized grips for higher or lower wrist positions as well. When you grasp the bow, you may notice a slight downward pull on your wrist because of the weight of the bow. This downward pull is less apparent when the bow is drawn back and the wrist bones compress and align with the arm and shoulder bones. The bow grip then takes on the function of supporting the bow hand in its average position.

Allow the bow grip to support your palm without any finger or thumb pressure. You should be able to feel whether the bow grip fits the natural angle of your hand or whether it forces your hand into an uncomfortable position. A coach might look for the proper angle from a safe side view as well. If the grip forces your hand out of its natural position, you may want to consider buying another grip (if it is replaceable) or adding some hard putty to the grip to adjust it to your desired feel. Be sure you've got the fundamentals of grip position correct and very consistent before replacing or modifying the bow grip.

Sometimes archers incorrectly hold the bow outside the designed parameters.

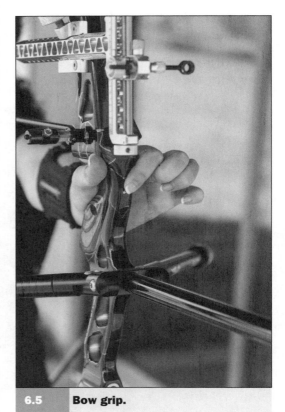

6.5 Bow grip.

Common problems with grip include holding the bow too high or too low. If the hand rises too high on the grip, the tendons strain and the wrist bones come out of alignment. If the hand is too low on the grip, an acute angle forms between the wrist and the arm, again forcing the wrist out of alignment and causing discomfort.

Of equal concern is pressure on the left or right side of the grip. If you are right-handed, gripping the bow too far on the left side of the grip will likely cause you to hit your arm with the bowstring. Too much pressure on the right side of the grip will cause discomfort in your wrist and hand. Both hand positions create torque, which affects the flight of the arrow and causes inconsistencies at the target.

For best results, find the correct pressure point and then tip your hand forward and apply it to the grip of the bow. Keep your thumb pointed toward the target and your first finger resting lightly on the front of the grip. Your remaining fingers should be curled under, with the knuckles pulled back toward you.

ANCHOR POINTS

The bow should be drawn back to the correct anchor point and no farther. The correct anchor point is determined by your level of archery experience, and must always be consistent.

If your first arrows are too long for your optimal draw length, it's okay to have them hang out in front of your bow a little. In fact, there should be some extra length as you adjust and find your correct draw length with strength and experience. It's better to develop proper shooting technique at this point; once you've become a consistent archer, work with your coach or local retailer to have your arrows custom fitted to your proper draw length.

The traditional way to draw a recurve bow with the fingers is to hold two fingers under the nock and one finger above. This is called a split finger hook. Beginning archers, however, sometimes find this draw difficult. Beginners tend to pinch the fingers together because of lack of experience, which tends to pinch the nock and cause the arrow to fall off the arrow rest. Do this enough times, and you might just think that arrow will never stay in place! As with everything else, a proper draw is learned in stages. If the split finger hook isn't working for you, try three fingers under the nock, and when you're comfortable with that, move to two fingers under and one finger over the arrow nock.

Three fingers under. Begin with three fingers under the nock and draw the string back to the corner of your mouth. The fingers hook the string using the archer's groove (figure 6.6). Refer to chapter 4 for more on the archer's groove. This method of hooking the bowstring, drawing the bow, and anchoring is just as accurate at closer ranges, and it keeps the fingers from pinching the nock, which results in the arrow being more likely to remain on the arrow rest. This draw also allows you to aim down the shaft of the arrow to start. Always be sure to use the same anchor point shot after shot. The corner of your smile is the easiest anchor point to remember consistently when you are getting started in the sport.

Two fingers under. As your shooting distances increase somewhat, you'll find that with three fingers under you can't aim high enough to hit the target while maintaining correct body alignment. This is the time to switch to the split finger hook (figure 6.7). Once you can draw the bow consistently to the cor-

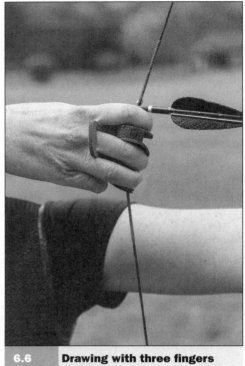

6.6 **Drawing with three fingers under.**

ner of your mouth using the split finger hook, and you're shooting consistent groups in the target, it's time to move your anchor down, to under your jaw. To accomplish this, take a minute to find your corner-of-the-mouth anchor point (without using your bow). Now, bring your hand straight down so that the fist knuckle of your index finger rests directly under your jawbone, and bring your hand slightly forward so that the second knuckle of your index finger is just below, and touching, the corner of your chin (figure 6.8). This is essentially the same hand position as the corner-of-the-mouth anchor point, but just with bone-on-bone contact between the hand and the jaw. The hand is just farther forward so that when you draw the bowstring, it comes to rest gently on the front of your nose and on the corner of your chin.

The bone-on-bone anchor point allows the arrow to sit lower when the bow is fully drawn, which effectively raises your aiming reference point, whether it is the point of the arrow or the aperture on your sight. It also allows you to hold a steadier anchor point because you are using your top finger rather than the arrow itself. Finally, this anchor point provides two key reference points: the bone-on-bone contact of your index finger knuckle under your jaw and the bowstring now touching the front of your nose.

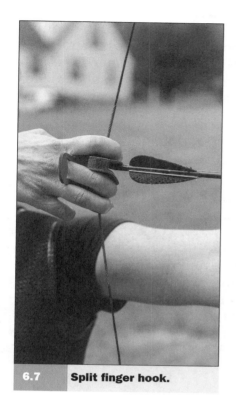

6.7 Split finger hook.

6.8 Anchoring under jaw with split finger hook.

Special finger tabs have been designed to make the most of this type of anchor. Often, a top ledge is built into the tab to hold it firmly underneath your lower jaw without interfering with your fingers. When using a ledge, it's important that you maintain solid contact between the top of your index finger knuckle and your jawbone. The ledge is simply for a reference; it should never be used as a substitute for bringing your hand into the proper position beneath your jaw.

Again, with this type of draw, hook your fingers deeply around the bowstring using the archer's groove. You might be tempted to draw the string using the tips of your fingers, but this causes a loss of back tension, which in turn creates major inconsistencies in your shot.

Consistent alignment is key to accuracy. In the beginning, it's enough to draw the bowstring to the same place under your jaw or at the corner of your smile. After you've gained some experience, you'll find yourself using the bowstring as part of that alignment by positioning it shot after shot in the same place—right on the tip of your nose. Most top competitors use this alignment technique. This alignment places your head and eyes in the same position for each shot. Because the string remains in front of your face where you can see it, there's little chance it will hit your face unless you turn your head suddenly during the shot. Positioning the string so that it touches your nose at full draw should only be done when you transition from three fingers under to a split finger hook. Combine this alignment technique with a solid anchor under your chin, with the top finger of your draw hand resting against the underside of your jawbone, and you've got a recipe for consistency and success.

Should you use this bowstring alignment method with a compound bow? It's really not necessary. For compound shooters using a mechanical release, once the bow is drawn back, the draw hand holding the mechanical release is often anchored under the jaw. However, because they often use a rear sight (also called a peep sight), that rear sight should be lined up with the aperture or scope, to present a completely clear picture and meet the natural position of the aiming eye. A misaligned peep sight can cause a multitude of form issues with regard to posture and head position that can extend into the shoulders and elbow. For this reason, be sure to have your peep sight set by your coach or local archery retailer.

Draw and Release

It's a misconception that archers stand still and shoot their bows. Proper shooting form helps you maintain bone-on-bone alignment through your hands, arms, and shoulders to provide needed stability, and your stance and posture create a stable platform. However, to achieve a consistent release and follow-through, some part of your body must always be in motion. The part of your body most likely to stay in motion with the greatest consistency is your back muscles. With proper training and plenty of practice, you can create a solid body alignment and use your back muscles (specifically, the lower trapezius) to draw the bow back and maintain back tension and direction of movement before releasing the arrow.

Think of your shoulder as a pivot point—your draw elbow and the back of your draw arm essentially rotate around the draw shoulder, powered by the movement of the back of the draw arm and the lower trapezius on the draw side of your back. When done properly, your draw-side scapula will actually move out and travel across the surface of your back toward your spine (figure 6.9). When you draw with your back muscles in this way, your drawing hand stays relaxed and your drawing arm doesn't have to carry the entire load. Combine this added relaxation and stability with the fact that your front sight is constantly in motion—finding its own center on the distant target—and your entire body becomes a relaxed aiming machine, with your body braced inside your bow and the bow an extension of your body.

If you continually try to draw the bowstring back using only your arm muscles, you will find that they quickly tire and that you can't count on your drawing arm to draw back the bowstring to the same position time after time. This kind of draw leads to what is called a collapse—a forward movement

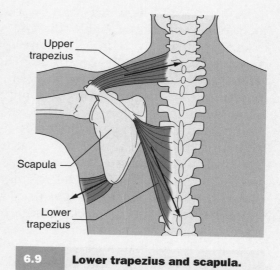

6.9 **Lower trapezius and scapula.**

of the back and arm muscles during the release of the bowstring, which has a detrimental effect on the body as well as the shot. To understand a collapse, imagine your release hand, draw-side elbow, and back muscles moving slightly forward in the direction of the target. In this unfortunate scenario, as the arrow is released, the arm and draw hand move slightly forward, and the draw hand opens and lets go of the bowstring instead of pulling properly through the release. If you are right-handed, this will result in arrows that are generally inconsistent and often low or to the right of the target.

You must maintain tension in the back of your draw arm and in your draw-side scapula (lower trapezius). This starts as a bigger movement during the early parts of the shot sequence and becomes slower and smaller as you get to the final steps of shooting.

If you are a compound shooter using a mechanical release, make sure that while your hand is hooking the release aid and your wrist and forearm are engaged, the back of your draw arm and lower trapezius are still moving in the same manner as they would to draw a recurve bow. If you allow your wrist to relax and stretch during the draw, serious injury could result. The back takes on the weight of the draw, and once you have anchored, keeps the arrow in an ever-so-slight backward motion until its actual release. This motion is subtle and is often no longer consciously noticed by the experienced archer. Rather, on a compound bow, this can be referred to as pulling against the wall, which refers to continuing your back tension and direction of movement even when you have hit the wall that is created by reaching your full draw length on the bow.

Release and follow-through should be thought of as natural consequences of proper back tension, whether shooting a recurve or a compound bow. That is, when your back is loaded with proper tension, your lower trapezius is bearing much of the weight of the shot, and you continue moving slowly in the same direction even when you've reached your anchor point, the release will become almost a subconscious act after consistent practice. Think about a compound bow: As your finger or thumb rests on the trigger after reaching full draw, and you continue to pull the string back against the wall, what activates the release aid? Not an increase of pressure on the trigger; rather, the *back pulls the draw arm*, which pulls the finger back against the trigger until the release occurs. As it occurs, the tension in the back continues to pull the draw arm and hand backward as the arrow is released from the bow.

Similarly, for a recurve bow, after reaching the anchor point and aiming for just a couple of seconds, you must "pull through" the release of the bowstring, relaxing the fingers as they continue the same back movement and direction with which they drew the bow. The draw hand and arm, and the draw side of the back, continue to move in the same direction as the arrow is released. This backward movement after the shot, whether on a compound or recurve bow, is called follow-through. It is important to note that you should maintain your stance and posture during the follow-through when shooting either type of bow. Do not lean backward or change your weight distribution; instead, keep the center of your body stable during the release and follow-through.

Remember, unlike a recurve bow, the compound bow is designed to let off its draw weight after a specific and predetermined distance of draw. The let-off often occurs in a very narrow window, and if the draw length position is not properly adjusted for you, let-off will be ineffective at best, and could lead to injury at worst. You need the assistance of a coach or archery expert to establish your proper draw length and adjust the draw length of your compound bow accordingly.

Only after you have learned the shooting sequence and can repeat it with proper shooting form should you have any expectation of holding a group at a target. If after shooting several ends (groupings of three or six arrows), you see that the arrows are hitting the target in random locations, your style is not yet consistent. If, however, the arrows are beginning to group on the target, regardless of where they are grouping, you are achieving a new level of consistency, which will eventually make you a successful archer. Remember, you can adjust your sight or aiming reference point to move your groups, but the groups must come first.

VISUAL AIDS

It's one thing to observe proper form in other archers, but it's quite another to feel it in yourself. You may feel that your alignment is perfect—that you're standing straight up and everything is where it should be. But without outside confirmation, you may be mistaken. It's always best to confirm what you feel with objective observations.

There are several ways to confirm your alignment. You can use your smartphone or a video camera to film two or three ends, and then review your form. Use a variety of angles when filming, but make sure the camera is in a safe location.

You can also use a full-length mirror. Position the mirror so you can see yourself without changing or interfering with your shooting form. A mirror provides real-time feedback on your form and posture. Bring your target very close so that you don't have to worry about missing it if you are busy studying your form. Right now you're correcting form, not accuracy.

An experienced archery instructor or coach is an invaluable tool for feedback. You can take just a lesson or two, or join an ongoing youth or adult club program, which will help you progress and eventually compete if you like. In either case, certified instructors and coaches are trained by USA Archery to detect subtle errors in form, and they can help you make positive changes.

On Target

Archery is a sport of repetition. With a standardized shooting technique, you can maintain consistency, resulting in tight groups on the target. Archery equipment is designed to fit the archer for maximum comfort and safety to achieve this consistency. It's possible to customize the equipment for greater comfort and control. Remember that every body is unique, so variations in style are to be expected.

7

CHAPTER

Taking Aim

Sight lines are straight; arrow paths are vertically curved. Even though you can look straight at a target, an arrow flies in an arc. The farther away the target is, the higher the arc is in most cases. The purpose of aiming is to ensure that the arc of your arrow and your line of sight meet at the target center. It sounds hard, but it's really quite instinctive. An experienced archery instructor or coach will tell you that although the aiming process is important, overconcentrating on aiming can cause your form and shooting sequence to suffer. If you keep in mind that aiming is one part of the overall process and not the sole goal of your shooting, you'll always shoot with confidence. If you're skeptical, think about this: No matter what their age, if you put people with no archery experience in front of a target and tell them to shoot, you'll rarely need to tell them to aim at the center. Human instinct drives us all to aim at the middle of the target. By focusing most of our energy on repeatable form, we allow the brain to automatically take over the aiming process, making aiming a simple task. This chapter offers some tips on aiming and demonstrates how to use some of the more common sights.

Instinctive Aiming

When an arrow is released toward the target, it fights gravity immediately, the same as a thrown ball. To hit a target, you need to aim a little higher (depending on the distance) than your line of sight, although when using a sight with an aperture on your bow, you might not notice it is aiming a little higher. Indoors, and on a calm day, this arc is pretty much the same shot after shot. The distance to the target as well as environmental factors such as altitude, wind, and rain, however, can change the shape of the arc. Practicing in various weather conditions and shooting in different geographical regions will accustom you to these variables.

Some archers shoot instinctively, whereas others use a point of reference, such as the point of the arrow, to aim. Pure instinctive shooting refers to looking at the target and taking the shot—literally using your instincts to feel the correct position in which to take the shot. Aiming without a front sight but with a reference point is still aiming, and not technically considered instinctive shooting, because a reference point is being used. Focus points differ among archers. Some archers focus on the target; others focus on the position of the tip of the arrow in relationship to the target. What you focus on isn't as critical as focusing on the same thing time after time.

Many archers shooting in archery programs initially learn to shoot by aiming using the point of the arrow, or by using a simple front sight. In the absence of a true, adjustable front sight, you can make a makeshift sight from a matchstick secured to the front of the riser with masking tape; you can move it up or down to compensate for your groups. Learning to shoot without an adjustable front sight has some advantages. First, it's easier to learn to shoot with good form when there is no sight to distract your eyes from the target. Second, it's easier on your instructor, who can coach without worrying about whether the sight is out of adjustment. If you purchased your new bow with a sight, you can choose whether to keep it in place and learn to use it right away or remove it until you've established consistent shooting form.

Instinctive archers often cant, or tilt, their bows (figure 7.1). This provides a little more solid feel on the arrow rest and slightly better visibility when aiming along the arrow. If you choose to cant your bow, however, keep in mind that canting is only one technique and not the way you should shoot at all times. It's difficult to cant the bow exactly the same way and to the same degree on each shot; and during a tournament or practice with others, canting can cause your bow to enter someone else's shooting space.

To shoot instinctively, it's important to develop a strong sight memory and good body awareness. The key to this type of shooting is to remember exactly what you were looking at and exactly how your body was positioned at the moment of release, shot after shot. If your shot placement was good, then recreate that placement from memory to execute the next shot. All things being equal, the second arrow should hit the target right on top of the first arrow. If the second arrow misses the mark, ask yourself what you might have done differently that time; resist the impulse to focus on the fact that you missed.

Instinctive aiming can be quite accurate at closer ranges, but you'll need to keep your expectations reasonable when shooting at more distant targets. Group sizes are generally larger (more spread out on the target) than they would be when using a sight. However, true instinctive archery (shooting without using a reference point for aiming, really learning to feel your shot) can greatly benefit your shooting form, because it places most of the focus on technique.

7.1   **Canting the bow.**

More to choose and use

FRONT SIGHTS

Mounting a front sight is the simplest way of adjusting your bow to improve accuracy. When aiming at a distant round target using a circular aperture known as a ring or ring pin on your front sight, your eye naturally tries to align the two. Remember, a front sight works only if your shooting form is consistent. Also, a sight needs to be mounted correctly so you can use it without changing your posture.

Experienced archers focus on the target and allow the front sight to become a bit blurry as they aim. If you follow the proper shooting form, your eye will naturally tend to center on the target as you release the arrow. The harder you try to force the sight onto the target and hold it there, the more it will seem to drift and the more likely you will be to miss the target altogether. Concentrating too much on aiming can lead to a loss of back tension (i.e., collapse), which can create poor habits that may prove difficult to fix. Rather than run this risk, keep your eyes focused on your target and keep your back strong; this will steady your bow arm and sight.

MOUNTING A FRONT SIGHT

Most factory-made bows, be they recurve or compound, have pre-drilled and tapped mountings for front sights. Manufacturers have universal industry standards for screw and bolt dimensions, so regardless of the brand of sight you purchase, its mountings should fit your bow. Inexpensive sights are often made from plastic, whereas more precise tournament sights are typically made from other materials, including aluminum, titanium, and carbon fiber (figure 7.2). Many high-end sights are machined to offer the precise performance that top archers demand.

You may have to partially assemble your sight before mounting it to your bow (figure 7.3). The mounting bracket attaches directly to your bow, and the adjustable aperture assembly attaches to the bracket. The aperture itself might be made from a ring with a bright metal pin or even a ring and pin with a fiber optic strand attached. The aperture assembly slides up and down a graduated rule that is used as a reference in adjusting the sight for distance. The sight may also be threaded to allow for side-to-side adjustments of the aperture—either to account for the natural position of your aiming eye or to adjust for windage. A major advantage of high-end sights is microadjustability; they may feature long mounting bars to position the front sight as far away from you as possible for greater fine-tuning ability.

Compound archers are permitted to use magnified lenses for aiming, and this part of the sight is called the scope; it is the counterpart to the nonmagnified aperture on a recurve sight. These scopes typically feature liquid-filled levels, which indicate when the bow is in a level

7.2 **Front sights.**

7.3   **Assembled and mounted sight.**

(straight) position. *Note:* Use a level to mount a sight for a compound bow that has a liquid level in the scope. The sight itself must be mounted level for the scope to give an accurate reading once it's installed.

REAR SIGHTS AND BOWSTRING ALIGNMENT

A rear sight, also called a peep sight, can be used on many compound bows, but it is not allowed in recurve competitions. On a compound bow, the peep sight is tied into the strands of the bowstring (figure 7.4). Your local archery pro shop or coach can install one. Its position on the bowstring should match up perfectly with your aiming eye without any change in your posture or head position.

Recurve tournament archers may be denied a rear sight, but that doesn't mean they don't have a rear aiming aid. By aligning the bowstring either with the sight itself or down the center of the riser, you have a reference point that effectively serves as a rear sight. As

7.4   **Rear sight.**

with the peep sight on a compound bow, it's important to maintain proper posture and head position while using this reference point and to remember that it is a secondary reference point. The process of aligning the string is done at the end of the anchoring step described in chapter 4, and the alignment is then maintained subconsciously while focusing on back tension and aiming.

Using a Sight

Now it's time to go to the archery range and get more familiar with the skill of using your sight(s). If you're using a front sight for the first time, you should expect your groups to be inconsistent. This is just your body telling you that something's different and that the shooting sequence needs to be relearned with the additional step of aiming with your sight. Also, keep in mind that just because the sight is mounted doesn't mean it's going to send arrows where you think it might. The sight requires adjustment to work effectively.

The aperture (front sight pin or ring) aligns with both your eye and the distant target. It shows line of sight, but it is positioned on the target where the arrow's arced flight path will end. In other words, you are aiming at what you want to hit, but the path to it is not necessarily a straight line. You need to sight in (i.e., adjust the sight according to your shooting and to the distance) to group your arrows consistently at a given distance.

The aperture can be adjusted up, down, left, or right. Moving the pin down actually raises the front of the bow and causes the arrows to hit higher on the target. Raising the pin causes the bow to point downward and the arrows to hit lower. Likewise, moving the aperture to the left causes the arrows to move farther to the right, whereas moving the aperture to the right causes the group to move to the left. Simply put: When adjusting the sight, follow the group. If the group is hitting right, adjust the sight to the right, and the group will begin to move left.

Now you're ready to shoot. Start by shooting at least three arrows at a close target (5 yards, maximum), and be sure that your arrows are hitting the target consistently. If the three arrows group somewhere on the target, regardless of where, you can be assured that your shooting form and the wind (if any) have been consistent.

Reposition your sight by "chasing the arrows" in the direction of the arrow group. Make all of your adjustments in small increments, and shoot the same arrows again. It is best to make one type of adjustment at a time—for example, first get the height correct, and then focus on left–right adjustments. If the arrows still group, and if they begin to group in the general area of your adjustment, then all is well. Continue adjusting your sight until the arrows group consistently at the center of the target. The sight adjustment is now good for that distance using the very arrows you shot. This is a great time to make a note of your sight mark so that you know how to position your sight when shooting that distance again. Remember, adjustments related to distance generally refer to height. If you switch arrows or place the sight on another bow, you must make the adjustments all over again. If you have other arrows in your collection, be sure to keep them separate from the rest.

After you have shot at the target at close range, begin moving the target back at increments until it is at a distance of 18 meters (20 yd), the distance used for indoor target archery tournaments, or until you are at the maximum range at which you can hit the center comfortably. Remember, the point of archery isn't to see how far away you can get from the target and still hit it. More important is to be able to hit the center consistently. Note the distance and record it in your notebook along with the sight position as found on the sliding sight bar. Some sights also have a sight tape, a blank tape along the side of the sight that allows you to make marks as to where your sight is positioned to hit a particular distance. If you decide to make a mark on the sight tape as well, be sure to use pencil so you can erase and remark as you progress. As you increase the distance, continue to adjust your sight up or down to ensure that the arrows continue to group at the target center. You'll notice that the farther back you are, the smaller the adjustments need to be to make a difference.

The wind is a constant factor in your use of a sight. A headwind causes the arrow in flight to slow down and drop sooner. A tailwind allows the arrow to maintain its speed longer, causing it to hit higher on the target. A crosswind pushes the arrow to one side, and an angled wind may affect several factors all at once.

With practice, you will learn how to judge the wind and predict the effect it will have on your arrows. Some archers adjust their sights consistently to account for the wind, thereby always keeping the aperture aimed at the center of the target. Others aim off, meaning that they leave the sight alone regardless of the wind direction and speed and adjust their aim away from the center of the target and farther in the direction the wind is coming from. Both techniques require practice and educated guesses. Aiming off is generally a better way to shoot because the wind is seldom steady. Outdoor tournament targets usually have small flags attached at the top to assist archers in observing shifting wind directions. However, it is important to note that the flags are not always accurate. In a field or stadium with walls or partial walls or with a tree line around the field, the wind may swirl and the flags may not provide a true reading. Therefore, it's important to get lots of practice in varying environmental conditions, so that you can learn how your shot and your bow behave under various conditions and determine which wind management techniques work best for you.

On compound bows, the peep sight is generally fixed into position on the bowstring, and all the sight adjustments are made to the front sight. When using a peep sight, be sure that it meets your aiming eye in the eye's natural position and that you are not leaning over to peek through it. The picture presented by the peep sight should be clear of string strands, and your scope or aperture should be centered within it. Changing your eye's natural viewing position to compensate for a poorly positioned peep sight can hurt your posture and shooting alignment, so enlist the help of a certified coach or archery retailer who can install the peep sight safely, make sure it's fitted properly to you, and then secure it to the bowstring by tying it in with serving thread. Remember to recheck your rear sight periodically to ensure that it's still tied in at the original position and has not moved on its own. If your groups suddenly become erratic, your peep sight may have shifted on the bowstring. If this is the case, rather than trying to fix it yourself, bring it to your local archery retailer or coach to get help. To install a peep sight, the bow has to be put into a bow press so that the peep sight can be inserted in the strands of the bowstring, and your posture and anchor point must be rechecked. It's important to have the help of someone who can accurately judge your form *and* safely reinstall the peep sight.

On a recurve bow, some archers use a kisser button, an additional nock locator that is installed above the nocking point and touches the archer's mouth when the bow is drawn to anchor (figure 7.5). The kisser button is unrelated to the aiming process except that it helps to keep your head in the same position shot after shot. Using a kisser button causes the aiming eye to remain in the same position in relation to the sight. This technique also reminds you to keep your drawing hand in the same position as you anchor under your jaw. At full draw, before you settle in to aim at the target, position the kisser button between your lips and the bowstring on the tip of your nose.

Keep in mind that a kisser button can present some issues. Primarily, as archers grow or as their draw lengths or form change, many begin to adjust themselves to the kisser button by tipping the head or leaning forward, rather than remembering to adjust the position of the kisser button on the bowstring. Additionally, some archers start to feel for the kisser button rather than focusing on the correct position of the draw hand at anchor, which can lead to other form and alignment issues. For this reason, a kisser button is not ordinarily recommended for most archers. It can be useful as a temporary aid for an archer who is having serious difficulty reaching the same anchor point each time. After that issue has resolved, however, the kisser button should be removed.

Kisser button

7.5 **Kisser button.**

Give it a go

SIGHT DRIFT

It is virtually impossible to hold your front sight on a distant target and keep the sight from moving around. Your body moves, your heart pulses, you get excited and get the shakes, the wind blows your bow around—these occurrences are a natural part of the process. Meanwhile, your objective is to remain confident and relaxed. Despite all the movement, your arrow will find its way to the center of your target, thanks to your focus on your back tension and proper direction of movement—and your brain's instinctive ability to aim.

Here's an easy drill that will reinforce this principle. Because the front sight is always in motion, the only way to limit the motion's effect on your accuracy is to concentrate on your total shooting form. To demonstrate this to yourself, have a partner stand to the side of you while you are at full draw. Your partner should always remain safely behind the shooting line but should have a full view of your profile. Concentrate on holding your front sight onto the target as strongly as you can and ask your partner to make note of any movement of your front sight as you count to 10.

Now, set down (i.e., bring the string slowly back toward the riser) and rest for several minutes. Come to full draw again and allow your sight to float around on the target, while concentrating on your muscle movement and bone-on-bone alignment. Set down again and relax. Ask your partner to compare the two sessions in terms of observable movement of the front sight. Your second session should have less sight movement. By focusing on your total technique, you'll learn to use your front sight as a guide in the process, while you stay focused on back tension and proper alignment.

WIND SHIFTS

One important thing to remember about shooting in the wind is that the wind will shift and change directions while you are shooting. You may take your cues from other archers on the field—for example, you may notice that everyone's at full draw when suddenly, like a row of dominoes, they all set down as the wind blows across the field. Also, the wind at one side of the field may be different from the wind at the opposite side, especially if there is a tree line on one side and the other side is open. Shooting in a variable wind (winds moving in different directions) is common.

Here's a great way to learn how to work with shifting winds. When shooting in a crosswind, adjust your sight until the arrows hit the target center. Shoot several ends while continuing to adjust the sight as needed to compensate for wind shifts and changing wind speeds. Record your group scores and the number of times you had to adjust your sight.

Now reposition your sight to where you had it marked prior to this exercise. Shoot several ends without adjusting the sight for wind, and aim off the target slightly to account for the changing wind drift. If the wind is blowing left to right, hold a bit farther left; then do likewise for the right. Which technique felt more natural? Many archers prefer to learn to aim off rather than try to make constant sight adjustments to the wind.

In general, it's important to remember to adjust your sight, whether shooting indoors or out, and especially during a tournament. Many archers forget or are unwilling to adjust their sights during a tournament and are dismayed to see an entire group of arrows in one place in the target at the end of the competition. When you know you've made two or three good shots and they are grouped together but not in the middle, adjust the sight. As you become a better and more experienced archer, you'll get a better feel for when the problem is the result of an error in technique and when a sight adjustment is in order.

On Target

Whole books, seminars, and archery schools are devoted to the subject of aiming. However, keep aiming in perspective. Although aiming is an important part of the process of shooting an arrow consistently, the most important area to focus on is your shooting form as a whole.

Maximizing Performance

This chapter discusses how to get the most accurate performance from your archery equipment. Many recreational archers are satisfied with the average performance of arrows they make or buy. But for archers who plan to compete, average performance doesn't win very often. For those archers, equipment selection and tuning become very important. Tuning refers to the process of determining the stiffness or weakness of the arrow shaft relative to the force applied by the bow. Making small adjustments to arrows and bow accessories to achieve optimal arrow flight is referred to as a good tune.

If you could watch your arrows flying to the target from the side, you might notice that they don't always follow a very straight path. Sometimes they appear to wiggle back and forth in flight before hitting the target. Likewise, you might occasionally see arrows sticking out of the target at odd angles even though you shot at the target straight on. This unwanted movement wastes kinetic energy and also makes it difficult to achieve tight groups. The ideal arrow is one that flies off the bow straight and hits the target squarely.

Troubleshooting

If your arrows hit the target in random positions, you should take a look at your shooting form again before you start working on equipment. Ask an instructor or coach to watch you shoot and help you adjust your form until your arrows are grouping somewhere on the target. However, if your arrows are grouping on the target (which means your form is consistent), but they are not grouping in the center of the target (figure 8.1), there are steps you can take to help get them to hit where you want.

Fortunately, it's possible to identify the flight characteristics of your arrows and to make some simple adjustments to make them fly straighter to achieve tighter, more centered groups (figure 8.2).

You may be wondering whether adjusting the sight as described in chapter 7 might help you center your groups. It may. However, if a pattern emerges over time in which most of your arrows, or most of the arrows that separate from the group, tend to go in the same direction, one or more of the common problems outlined in table 8.1 may be to blame. The solutions described in the pages that follow the table will help get you back on target.

8.1 Off-center arrow group.

8.2 Centered arrow group.

Table 8.1 Errors Associated With Off-Center Arrow Groups

High or low arrows

- Inconsistent anchor point
- Nocking the arrow incorrectly (relative to the nock locator)
- Holding the bow too high or low on the handle

High arrows

- Heeling the bow, or tipping it up; applying too much pressure with the heel of the hand
- Raising the bow arm upon release
- Drawing past the anchor point
- Lowering the draw hand upon release; pulling the string down
- Anchoring too low, rather than tight against the jaw
- Upward pressure from the hook onto the arrow
- Pushing through the shot with the bow arm, rather than using draw-side muscles

Low arrows

- Dropping the bow arm upon release
- Moving the head forward to meet the string when anchoring; shortening draw length
- Collapsing, or failing to maintain back tension
- Leaning toward the target
- Applying downward pressure from the hook onto the arrow

Left or right arrows

- Canting, or tilting, the bow to the left or right
- Gripping the bow too tightly, causing it to torque sideways in the hand
- Peeking at the target upon release; moving the head to see where the arrow landed
- Aligning the string incorrectly

Left arrows

Right-handed archers

- String hitting the chest, arm, or clothing upon release
- Aiming with the left eye

(continued)

Table 8.1 (*continued*)

Left-handed archers

- Pulling the draw hand away from the face upon release (known as plucking the string); opening the hand to release rather than pulling through the release
- Collapsing; moving the bow arm left upon release
- Grabbing the bow; tightening the grip upon release

Right arrows

Right-handed archers

- Pulling the draw hand away from the face upon release, known as plucking the string; opening the hand to release rather than pulling through the release
- Collapsing; moving the bow arm right upon release
- Grabbing the bow; tightening the grip upon release

Left-handed archers

- String hitting the chest, arm, or clothing upon release
- Aiming with the right eye

When making adjustments, always shoot at least two groups of arrows to verify the cause of the issue and the success of the adjustment you've made. Ideally, you should have a dozen identical arrows. Remove the fletching from two or three of the arrows. These unfletched arrows—called bare shafts—will be used as part of your tuning, as described later. Also, number each of your remaining arrows. If your groups are ruined by a single errant arrow, numbering the arrows will tell you whether the fault lies with your tuning or with a particular arrow that should be replaced.

To minimize bowstring contact, make sure your body posture is consistent, and wear fitted clothing. Also, use an arm guard and—especially for recurve shooting—a chest protector. Finally, be sure your nocks are always properly rotated so that the index fletching is properly positioned on each of your arrows. Failure to do so can result in inconsistent groups.

More to choose and use

INCONSISTENT ARROW FLIGHT PATH

Porpoising and fishtailing are terms used to describe arrows that move irregularly in flight in a manner that resembles the movements of these creatures of the sea. Both actions are symptoms of problems that are correctable. Porpoising is when the arrow moves up and down in flight (figure 8.3a). This usually occurs when the nock locator is positioned too high or low on your bowstring, resulting in incorrect nock height. You can tell that your arrows are porpoising when they hit the target with their ends pointed up or down. The nock locator on your bowstring can be adjusted up or down to correct for porpoising. You'll need two tools to correct nock height: nockset pliers and a bow square. First, take a measurement with your bow square to see where the nock locator is positioned, and take note of the measurement so that you have an idea of where you began. With the bow square clipped all the way onto the bowstring, and the long part of the bow square resting on the arrow rest, the nock locator should be positioned at approximately 3/8 inch (1 cm) above level.

If the nock locator is not in that position, or if it is in that position but your arrows are still porpoising, you can try to correct the nock height. Loosen the locator with nockset pliers and slide it up or down the bowstring, making only very slight adjustments of 1/8 inch (0.3 cm) or less. If the nock locator is not at 3/8 inch (1 cm), start by bringing the locator closer to that position and see if that corrects the issue, before making any other adjustments.

If additional adjustments are needed, move the locator up the string to counter arrows hitting the target with their ends pointing up, and move the locator down the string to counter arrows whose ends are pointing down.

Fishtailing is a side-to-side movement of the arrow in flight (figure 8.3b). This issue is easily identified by seeing the nock of the arrow

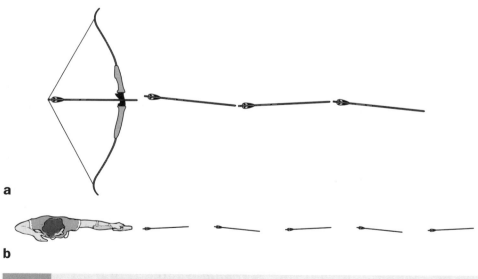

a

b

8.3 *(a) Porpoising and (b) fishtailing.*

moving side to side as the arrow travels to the target. Fishtailing is usually caused by an improper tune, meaning that the arrows are either too stiff and don't flex enough or too weak and flex too much. Be sure to make nock height adjustments first, prior to correcting for fishtailing. In general, make all of your adjustments in small increments and verify these adjustments by shooting additional arrows without moving your sight. In other words, you're looking for consistency in a group of arrows, not to hit the center of the target.

All of the corrections for porpoising and fishtailing need to be made at the archery range. When making corrections, be sure to document as much as you can, and maintain consistent shooting form at all times.

ADJUSTING CENTER SHOT

If the arrow is hitting the target to the right or left, check your center shot (the alignment of the arrow in relationship to the centerline of the limbs and bowstring). It may be misaligned. If your recurve bow has a plunger, start by standing the bow up and look at it from behind the bowstring and nocked arrow, so that you can look down the line of the bowstring. It should be roughly centered on the top and bottom limb. Check to see where the arrow point is relative to the bowstring when all is aligned. If the point of the arrow is far left or right of the bowstring, adjust the plunger in or out, and reinspect the position of the arrow point to ensure that it appears centered, or just outside of center, relative to the bowstring. With a compound bow, adjust the movable arrow rest for the same effect.

Take it to the range

Tuning Your Equipment

Tuning a recurve bow is different from tuning a compound bow. Recurve bows may have adjustable or nonadjustable arrow rests, and some recurve bows have an adjustable plunger installed. A compound bow doesn't use a plunger, but the arrow rest itself is often adjustable.

One process for tuning your recurve bow is called bare-shaft tuning, arguably the most reliable method of tuning there is. Do not begin the process of tuning, with a bare shaft or otherwise, until you are comfortable with your shooting technique and are shooting consistent groups in your target at the distance you would shoot in a beginner competition. If your shooting form is inconsistent, tuning will quickly become a frustrating exercise.

First, you need two arrow shafts that have nocks and points installed, identical to your fletched arrows, but without fletching. If all of your arrows have feathers or vanes on them, take a minute to remove the vanes or feathers from two arrows.

There are a couple of things to look for when bare-shaft tuning a bow: placement of the bare shaft, and the angle at which the shaft enters the target relative to the position of the nock. Additionally, adjusting your nock height can affect the way the arrow behaves relative to spine, so focus on making any height adjustments before beginning to analyze and correct for spine.

Placing your target 10 yards away, shoot three or four fletched arrows followed by two unfletched arrows. Both groups should hit the target in the same position. If the unfletched arrows are higher than the fletched arrows, you'll know your nock locator is still too low on your bowstring and should be moved up slightly. Likewise, if the unfletched arrows are lower than the fletched arrows, then the nock locator is too high on the bowstring and should be moved down slightly. At this point, even if your nock height started at the recommended 3/8 inch (1 cm) above level, it's now okay to change it, because the bare shaft is telling you that, for whatever reason, the nock locator is too high or low for you.

Although recurve tuning takes time and experience to learn—and is not an exact science—the bare shaft will tell you quite a bit about whether your arrows are too weak, too stiff, or just right for you. If you are right-handed and using a recurve bow, unfletched arrows that hit to the right of the fletched arrows generally means that the spines of the arrows are weak, though there are exceptions to this rule. You can increase the spring tension of your plunger slightly to make them fly stiffer. Likewise, if the bare shaft arrows land to the left of the group (again, if you are right-handed), decrease the spring tension on the plunger to make the arrows tune a bit weaker. The angle at which the bare shafts enter the target is equally important as where the bare shafts land. For a right-handed archer, a bare shaft that enters the target to the left of its nock indicates a stiff tune, whereas a bare shaft entering the target to the right of its nock is weaker. To adjust your plunger, you usually have to loosen a set screw on the plunger and then turn the bolt at the back of the plunger using an Allen wrench. However, check the instructions that came with your plunger for complete information.

Continue to make your corrections until the fletched and unfletched arrows hit the target at roughly the same location. Then, move the target back to 20 yards and repeat the corrections. Generally, you will get the most reliable bare-shaft tuning results at a maximum distance of 30 yards. Beyond that, even if you are regularly shooting a tournament distance that is beyond 30 yards, it is best to see how the arrows group and work with your coach on advanced tuning techniques. A number of factors could affect the tune of your bow: arrow shaft, nocks, point weight, brace height, string material—the list goes on and on. Be sure to keep note of your equipment setup at the time you tune, and then retune if you make adjustments to your archery equipment.

Paper-tuning yields similar results for compound archers, but is done at a closer range and using only fletched arrows. Basically, a blank sheet of paper is supported by a frame placed a few yards directly in front of you. You shoot fletched arrows through the paper into a target that is directly behind the paper. Instead of noting where the arrows hit on the target, you inspect the paper sheet and note the direction of the tears made by the passing arrows. Paper-tuning is recommended for compound bows, and reading a tear should be done with someone who has the training and knowledge to adjust your bow appropriately. Be sure to work with your local archery retailer or certified coach when it's time to paper-tune your compound bow. As with a recurve, remember that changes to your bowstring, arrows, and arrow rest will all change the tune of your bow, so be sure to get your bow paper-tuned anytime a change is made.

The equipment adjustments described here assume that you have chosen the right arrows for your particular equipment based on the arrow manufacturer's recommendations. If, after numerous attempts to adjust the plunger (or compound bow arrow rest), you find that the arrows continue to have flight issues, such as porpoising or fishtailing, and your groups do not reflect your level of skill and experience, the arrows may not be properly matched to your equipment in terms of their stiffness—or you may have a form issue that is causing problems with your arrow flight. Review the arrow manufacturer's selection chart to make sure you have the correct arrows for your particular bow. You may find that the arrows you have are not suitable for your equipment, and you may be faced with purchasing new ones.

However, before purchasing new arrows, have someone with tuning experience help you read the bare shaft relative to the groups, as well as oversee the corrections you're making. Tuning correctly requires a wealth of experience and knowledge, and although you need to start somewhere in terms of learning how to tune, it's best learned with an experienced coach who can help you along the way. Additionally, the coach can help spot any form-related issues that may be impacting your tuning session.

If a new equipment purchase becomes necessary, remember that it is possible, under the right circumstances, to alter the tune of an arrow by changing your draw weight, the length of the arrow shaft, the weight of your arrow points, or the type of nock you use. Other adjustments, such as changing the type of bowstring material and number of strands in the bowstring, may help alter the spine as well. Remember, however, that increasing your draw weight to weaken the spine of your arrows is not a recommended tuning method, unless you are ready to increase your draw weight, having developed good physical strength after consistent practice, and a truly consistent archery technique. As a rule, these tuning adjustments should be done with the guidance of a certified archery coach or retailer.

Give it a go

PLOTTING YOUR GROUPS

Once you've finished bare-shaft tuning your recurve bow or paper-tuning your compound bow, it's time to decide which setups work best for you. As you become a more advanced archer, you may experiment with weights on the bow, such as a front stabilizer or side rod(s), different types of fletching on your arrows, or new nocks. To determine whether new equipment is really beneficial to you, try plotting.

A plot sheet, which you can make yourself, is essentially a piece of paper with several small archery targets on it. For each end you shoot, note which equipment variation you used, and then mark on the targets where the groups landed. To get good results, be sure you are sufficiently warmed up before you start, and don't change your sight during the exercise.

Alternate between your existing setup and the new equipment option, end after end. For example, you might be shooting three arrows fletched with feathers and three arrows fletched with vanes, to see which ones fly and group better for a 20-yard tournament. Plot each group carefully, and then at the end of your practice, you can see which type of equipment produced tighter groups.

There are also a number of apps available that offer plotting capabilities. These apps can be handy for tracking equipment performance, evaluating equipment and form changes, and tracking your practice and tournament progress.

ARROW NODE TAP

In flight, an arrow tends to wiggle back and forth on two balance points called nodes—one toward the front of the arrow near the point, and the other near the back of the arrow by the vanes. How do you know where the arrow nodes are? You can find them with a simple tap.

Hold an arrow lightly by the nock and allow it to hang down. Now tap the side of the arrow and feel the vibration through your fingers. It will die down almost at once. Move your fingers down in front of the vanes and tap again. The vibration will last longer. Move your fingers back and forth along that area and keep tapping until you find the place where the vibration lasts the longest. This is the location of the rear node. Repeat the drill at the front of the arrow to locate the front node.

On Target

Achieving tight arrow groups is a matter of deliberate and calculated testing and adjusting—of both shooting technique and mechanical equipment. Knowing why your arrows behave the way they do is critical to knowing how to correct their flight characteristics. With your equipment adjusted to perform at its best, you'll get more enjoyment from your time shooting, and hopefully better tournament scores.

Scoring

Now that you've learned how to shoot, what are you going to shoot at? Archery targets come in lots of shapes and sizes, each designed for a particular type of game, referred to in archery as a round. Archery targets are generally made up of two parts. The part you shoot at to score is called the target face. The part that you hang the archery face onto is called the target butt or target mat. Use special target pins—or long, thick nails—to secure your target face to the mat. In the case of a 3D foam target with the scoring rings molded in, or if you use a stuffed target bag with the scoring rings printed on it, there is no separate target face.

Scoring a Target

Archery targets are generally round with distinctly marked circles indicating the scoring zones (figure 9.1, *a* and *b*). The closer to the center of the target you hit, the higher the score. If the arrow hits the target right on the line between two scoring colors, as long as the arrow is touching the scoring line, count the higher score. If an arrow passes through the target or bounces out, often all that's left is a hole or mark where the arrow originally hit; in that case, score the hole, provided that the archer has been marking each arrow in the target (discussed later in this chapter).

When you go to the target to score your arrows, it's important not to touch the arrows or target until all arrows in the target are called (i.e., assigned a score value) and all scores are recorded on scorecards. It may be tempting to wiggle an arrow around to get a better look or to try to get it to touch another scoring line, but this is a violation of rules in almost all archery organizations and will get you disqualified from the tournament. Also, moving arrows on a target is not ethical sporting behavior and will make you a very unpopular shooting partner. Leave all the arrows in place. Once you or someone else in your scoring group assigns a score value to each arrow, add up all the scores from your arrows and write them down before pulling them out of the target. If you're shooting with a partner and are keeping score, you'll need to be in full agreement about all

9.1 *(a)* **Multicolored archery target and** *(b)* **target face commonly used for scoring indoor archery tournaments.**

the scores before pulling the arrows out. During a tournament, the other archers in the scoring group must verify and agree with the proposed scoring before the arrows are removed.

If your arrow bounces out of or passes through the target, or becomes embedded in another person's arrow, you receive the score value of the arrow's hole or of the damaged arrow in the target. These are general guidelines, however, and the official rules of a tournament may state otherwise.

Official scorecards are usually provided at tournaments. Sample scorecards (figure 9.2), based on scoring standards set by USA Archery and World Archery, are often available at archery ranges and

Event logo   Event name
                    Event location   Archer label
                    Event dates

End	1	2	3	End score	Running score
1					
2					
3					
4					
5					
6					
7					
8					
9					
10					
11					
12					
13					
14					
15					
16					
17					
18					
19					
20					
Total: 60 arrows					

_____
Scorer signature

_____
Scorer signature

_____
Archer signature

Score summary	Score	10	9
Totals			

9.2 Sample scorecard.

Courtesy of USA Archery.

pro shops. They are also available from the archery organizations themselves (see the resources section). There are several columns and blocks under each column. Each time you score a group of arrows, it is called an end. Typically, each end has either three or six arrows. In this example, we'll use a three-arrow end. Note that our sample scorecard has room for 20 ends, which makes this a 60-arrow tournament, otherwise known as a 600 round or 60-arrow round. Use one column to record the total score for the arrows shot during each end (i.e., the subtotal of the end, called the end score) and another column to record the running score (i.e., the combined score for all the ends shot so far). As you count the scores of your arrows that are still in the target, count the highest-scoring arrow first and write it down in the left box; then write down the second-highest arrow in the middle box; and finally, record the lowest-scoring arrow in the right box. Add the scores near the bottom of the card. The total end scores should agree with the total running score. Make sure to complete the full scorecard.

When you're through with all the ends, calculate your final score. Tournament rules vary as to the number of ends you shoot and the number of arrows shot per end. You can judge your performance by comparing your score with the total possible score for that particular target. Calculate the total possible score for the tournament by multiplying the number of arrows shot by the maximum score allowed per target. For example, 60 arrows shot multiplied by a maximum possible score of 10 per arrow equals a total possible score of 600. This method is the very best way to measure your growth in the sport in terms of your scoring potential; however, you should set goals that are reasonable for your level of experience and not feel discouraged if your score is a long way from perfection. The reality is that it takes archers years to achieve a perfect score, and in fact, most never do. This is part of the fun of archery—there's always a new challenge to conquer! The good news is that if you continue to practice and keep score occasionally, you'll learn what to expect of yourself, and enjoy the fun of setting new personal best objectives that are just beyond your current level.

More to choose and use

MARKING A TARGET

Archery targets can quickly get covered with arrow holes, which makes it difficult to judge whether an arrow pass-through is yours. If you are serious about keeping score during a particular round, it's advisable—and sometimes required—to mark your target face, beginning with the first practice arrow you shoot. You do this by using a pencil or pen to draw a short straight line next to each arrow you've scored, prior to pulling it from the target (figure 9.3). After all the arrows have been removed, you can easily see where each arrow has hit; and, if another arrow then passes through the target, you'll be able to identify—and score—its hole because it's not yet marked. Of course, when shooting in a competition, be sure to review the rules regarding marking arrow holes during the event before you begin scoring.

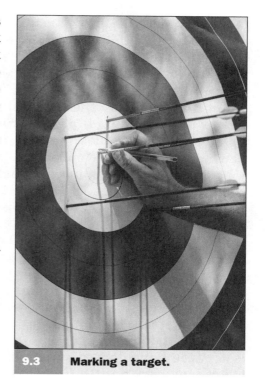

9.3 **Marking a target.**

SELECTING TARGET FACES

Target faces are made from several materials—heavy paper, reinforced paper such as Tyvek, and even a very durable and waterproof plastic—and are available from a number of sources.

The target faces used in tournaments put on by an archery organization have a logo or emblem indicating that they are the official target faces of that organization and adhere to the rigid printing dimensions and standards set by the organization. In addition to scoring rings, some target faces may come with a small X printed in the center. X counts are still tallied in some tournaments to determine the most accurate archer; however, again, rules vary according to the type of competition. If you plan to compete against other archers, it's best to get the official target for that game and make sure you are very familiar with it.

Visit your local archery retailer to select a variety of target faces for your practice range. Your instructor or coach can explain the uses for each target and its scoring values. It's fine to use inexpensive or previously used faces when shooting on your own. Mount each target face in turn onto your target mat and practice shooting at it. Shooting at different types of target faces is great fun. If your target faces include an X in the center, for example, keep track of your count. Shooting the dead center of the target—the X—is sometimes referred to as killing the spider. Using different faces can really help to keep you excited about practice sessions. If you typically shoot a 40-centimeter (16 in.) target face at 18 meters (20 yd) all the time, change it up and try the National Field Archery Association (NFAA) indoor five-spot target face, or try your hand at 3D. Mixing things up is a great way to learn about other styles of archery and to find new ways to enjoy the sport!

Many types of target faces are used in archery. Following are four commonly used faces.

Multicolored (Olympic style). This is the target face that just about anyone would recognize (figure 9.4). It has 10 concentric scoring rings that are worth 1 through 10 points, with five colors—gold, red, blue, black, and white—and is used in the Olympic and Paralympic Games. It's also used in other target archery competitions. The five-color target comes in various metric diameters, again depending on the scoring game, ranging from about 122 centimeters (48 in.) to 40 centimeters (16 in.). Another variation on this target is a three-color target with five rings; it scores 10, 9, 8, 7, or 6 points, with anything else scored as a miss. This target face is generally used for compound rounds shot at 50 meters (55 yd) at outdoor tournaments. A similar face is used for target archery tournaments of shorter distances.

Field archery target faces. Field archery is often a simple scoring game with simple targets to match. Often, the official targets have just two colors—black and white—with three scoring circles, scoring 5, 4, and 3 points, consecutively. Again, this is a simple version of an NFAA target face, and others may look different according to the scoring game.

9.4 **Multicolored (Olympic-style) target.**

Multispot targets. Here's where archery competition really takes off. Target faces that come with multiple spots, or scoring zones, on each sheet are frequently used for indoor archery. Each target face may have anywhere from three to five spots (figure 9.5). Often, when using such a target, you get only one shot per spot. This restriction makes shooting more interesting because you are no longer shooting toward the center of a single target but have to subtly shift from target to target on what may be a very small sheet.

9.5 **Multispot target face.**

Three-dimensional (3D) target scoring. The term *3D* is generally used for any target that's molded into the shape of an animal. The scoring circles are molded into the target in a position that would indicate an approximate kill zone in the live animal. 3D target shooting is very popular. Not only does it require highly refined technical form, but also distances must be judged accurately because the targets are frequently placed along a roving path at unknown distances, often in the woods or in rough terrain. The sport is intended to simulate bowhunting; the archer faces the challenges of maintaining shooting form, judging distances, confronting confusing shadows that may fall across the target, and assessing the color of the target, which may be different according to the species of animal.

Take it to the range

Target Mats and Stands

Target mats used to be made primarily from natural grasses woven in a circle or square, wrapped in canvas, and sewn tightly. You can still buy grass mats, and they are popular because of their relative low cost and availability, although they can be costly to ship. Stacked bales of hay work well, too.

Foam has become the target mat material of choice because of its greater durability and weather resistance. Often, mats are made by rolling long strips of foam into a circle and binding the final strip to secure the wrap. In this way, an arrow doesn't have to pierce the foam itself to stop; it just forces its way between layers. Many foam target mats offer replaceable cores that can be punched out and replaced with a new center section should it get too mushy from multiple arrow hits. In this way, foam retains its value longer than grass does, and is often used at target archery tournaments because of its durability.

Archery practice ranges can be set up in minutes with many of the new portable bag-and-block targets on the market today. Target manufacturers offer a variety of foam blocks with target faces painted on them. Also, bags made from synthetic cloth and filled with foam or even cloth rags can be suspended from frames and used as practice targets.

Portable stands are often used by archery clubs and programs, and when the target positions are moved frequently or the field is multiuse and accommodates other sports. Stands can be made from wood and may have wheels, which offer greater ease in terms of target movement and field setup. A quick Internet search turns up lots of suggestions on building a target stand that is durable and movable. Bear in mind that wooden stands and target mats themselves are heavy, and it may take two or more people to move or transport a target mat that is attached to a stand. Rather than risk injury, take the mat off the stand and move it separately; you may find it easiest to roll the mat. A folding stand, of course, is easier to move than one that can't be folded.

Permanent target houses are used if the position of the target is fixed, as is often the case with field archery. The distance to the target is changed by moving the archer, not the target. The target house provides protection from the weather and sun and holds the target mat in position (figure 9.6).

9.6   **Permanent target house.**

ESTABLISHING AND SURPASSING YOUR AVERAGE

Archery is a game of repeatable motion. It's also a game of repeatable scores. If you shoot in a tournament, your only goal should be to make sure your form is consistent, and to focus on any form areas or mental training aspects you're currently working on. In practice, however, you can definitely prepare to shoot the same scoring rounds you'll shoot at tournaments. Your typical practice session should include working on personal form development followed by a practice round, using the format of whatever competition you plan to attend. Recording your scores from each practice round will give you a sense of the average score you're capable of shooting.

You can measure future practice rounds against your average, but this should not be the focal point of your shooting. Whenever you exceed your average, record what might have been the reason; then try to duplicate it during your next practice round. After your tournament is over, you can compare your tournament score with your practice average—but never do it while you are competing. Objectively record what may have caused you to shoot higher or lower than your practice average, and discuss the results with your instructor or coach. After you've competed in several tournaments, you'll get a sense of how you perform under pressure, and you'll be able to tailor your practice plans based on that.

SCORING IN CIRCLES

This exercise is great as a fun challenge once you've become confident and consistent in scoring on a single-spot target face. Depending on the game, the target face you shoot at may have one or more scoring circles, or spots. Important skills are not only hitting at the center of a target, but also being able to adjust your aim should there be more than one spot on that target. If you don't have a multispot target face to shoot at, simply stick three to five large, easily visible adhesive tape pieces onto your target face in a loose circular pattern (keep away from the target edges). These will be your new aiming spots.

Shoot one arrow at each aiming spot. Maintaining proper shooting form is critical for accuracy and consistent arrow grouping at each aiming spot. With practice, you should be just as accurate shooting at the multispot target as at the single-spot target.

On Target

Archery is a very easy sport to learn, but it demands a high degree of precision. That precision is what makes scoring such a challenge for both the new archer and the seasoned expert. The sport has evolved to include a wide variety of targets and games as well—making it fun for archers of all skill and experience levels.

Equipment Maintenance and Repair

Maintaining and repairing your equipment go hand in hand. Archery equipment can be a sizable investment, and the extra attention you give it can improve both its performance and its usable life span. Inspecting your equipment frequently can also aid in identifying any subtle changes that will eventually affect its safe use as well as its performance. Identifying changes early allows you to make small repairs as the need arises so that you can avoid a serious break that might permanently damage your equipment or, worse, cause injury to you or someone nearby.

Bow Inspection

Recurve risers and limbs can be made from a variety of materials. Many risers are made of aluminum or carbon; limbs can be made from carbon, wood, foam, or fiberglass and are frequently made from some combination of these materials. Limbs are often manufactured by laminating various types and layers of material together. The materials used to make recurve risers and limbs continue to evolve with technological advances in the sport of archery as archers and manufacturers pursue stability, accuracy, and speed as well as a smooth draw. Regardless of composition, the process of inspecting for safety is much the same for all bows.

Drawing the bow back to shoot an arrow causes flexing of the limbs. As long as this flexing follows the curve of the bow and does not torque the bow sideways, the adverse stress is minimal and the bow should last for years. However, undue stress may result if the bow is routinely drawn back farther than its design intended, or if it's ever drawn and released with no arrow, an action known as dry firing. Dry firing releases all of the bow's energy back into its limbs instead of into an arrow, and can result in broken limbs or injury.

Modern bow design takes normal flexing stress into account, and most bows will last for years if they are strung properly and stored in dry, temperature-controlled conditions. Before and after using your bow, always inspect it for damage or wear. Check the limbs for layers of material that appear to be splintering, separating, or de-laminating; examine all screws and bolts for tightness; and inspect the handle and the arrow rest for wear. Arrow rests can be replaced when worn, and bows with shelves that double as arrow rests (on inexpensive fiberglass camp bows, for example) can be rebuilt and shaved square again, provided they have a rubber shelf to shave. Do not, however, shave the fiberglass itself.

Also, inspect the string notches at either limb tip of the bow for any sharp edges that could catch on the bowstring. On an inexpensive takedown wooden bow, any roughness can be lightly smoothed with the careful use of sandpaper. Sand very gently, making contact only with the rough area and not the surrounding finish. Small pieces of laminate from the limb tips or handle may be reattached with epoxy glue. However, if your intermediate or high-end takedown bow has suffered from delamination of any kind, bring the bow to your local retailer for possible repair and to inquire about any warranty that may apply.

Fiberglass bows are prone to splintering, and when that happens, the best thing to do is to dispose of it. Fiberglass dust can be toxic, so although sanding a very shallow splinter is theoretically feasible, the fiberglass dust is very harmful. Any splinter can compromise the structural integrity of the bow, increasing the risk of a serious accident and injury. When in doubt, throw it out.

Splinters on a wood or laminate limb, such as on a takedown bow, should be cause to bring the bow to your local archery retailer for repair or replacement, performed under warranty if applicable. Under no circumstances should you try to repair a split, cracked, or splintered limb, or one that has delaminated (layers of the limb are coming apart). Depending on the bow, doing so could void your warranty and, again, could compromise the safety of the bow.

Any splinters, cracking, or delamination on a compound bow should be cause to bring the bow to your archery retailer immediately. Never attempt to repair a compound bow. Because the bow is under a greater amount of stress than a strung recurve bow, an unsuccessful attempt to repair it can lead to a serious accident resulting in injury. Additionally, most recently manufactured compound bows have a warranty that may be voided if you attempt to repair them yourself. Head to your retailer and get professional help to be sure the bow is safe to shoot and ready to perform at its best for you.

Next, inspect the bowstring on your recurve bow or the string and cables on your compound bow. A bowstring is made up of a series of strands. All strands should be intact. If a strand is broken, replace the string. Also, if the string as a whole has taken on a fuzzy appearance, it means that the original bowstring wax has rubbed or dried off and the strands are moving against each other rather than as a unit. Apply bowstring wax (beeswax) along the entire surface of the bowstring and work it into the string by rubbing it with a clean cloth or your fingers until the wax penetrates all the strands. Bowstrings and cables should be waxed weekly, or when they stop feeling tacky. Remember to wax the string and cables only, and never the served areas, especially the end serving; otherwise, wax can work its way into the compound bow cams and wheels, which can compromise the performance of the bow and present a potential safety hazard.

Finally, inspect the servings on the bowstring. The ends of the servings should be tight, and the serving itself should show few signs of wear. Usually, if a bowstring is damaged along its length, it's best to replace it. If the serving is damaged, loose, or unraveling, however, it's possible to make a short-term emergency repair until you can head to your local archery pro shop to have the serving replaced.

Note that this emergency repair is designed only to protect the serving and bowstring until you can get to an archery store for repair; it should not be expected to last for more time than it takes to finish your tournament and get it repaired professionally. You can definitely learn to make your own bowstrings, serve them, and repair servings. However, this is a skill that should be taught in person, making use of a bowstring jig, the proper string and serving materials, and a serving tool.

For an emergency repair that must be made in the field, follow these instructions:

1. Note the condition of your serving. A loose or unraveling thread is a sign that the serving needs repair (figure 10.1). The key to making this repair successful is to notice a frayed serving when it's still fairly far away from the nocking points—in other words, that the serving has just begun to unravel. If the serving has unraveled to the point where it is within an inch or less of the nocking point, do not repair it yourself. Instead, swap the bowstring out for your backup one, and leave the repair to the professionals.

| 10.1 | Serving thread coming unraveled. |

2. You will want the following emergency supplies in your archery kit to bring to tournaments: cyanoacrylate (CA) glue and sewing thread.

3. Identify the spot where the serving is coming unraveled. Grasp the loose end of the serving and pull it taut to the bowstring. Then cut a 6-inch (15 cm) length of your sewing thread. Tie it once onto the serving approximately 1/4 inch (0.6 cm) before the unraveling begins—where you have about 1/4 inch of solidly served string remaining before it unravels. Begin a process of tying, wrapping both ends around the string, and retying—approximately 10 rotations—working your way back up the serving (figure 10.2) until you have passed the end of the unraveling point by 1/4 inch, and there is no serving thread left under your wraps.

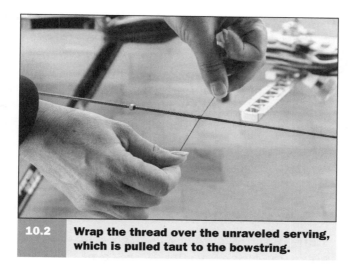

10.2 Wrap the thread over the unraveled serving, which is pulled taut to the bowstring.

4. When you get to the end spot, be sure to tightly double-knot once, wrap once more, and tightly double-knot again. Trim off the excess leaving just enough that you don't cut the knot itself. Use your finger to lock down the repair with a few drops of cyanoacrylate glue applied to your double knots and the wrapped thread just before it. *Note*: Cyanoacrylate glue bonds quickly.

Arrow Inspection

Arrows can hit a target with incredible force, and as a result they are subject to wear and breakage. Always inspect your arrows frequently while on the range. Check them over every time you pull them from a target. Ensure that they have tightly glued vanes or feathers, tightly glued points, and well-secured nocks. Also, inspect for any broken nocks or cracks or splits along their lengths. Finally, examine them for straightness. Wood arrows have a tendency to warp if they are kept in humid conditions. Fiberglass arrows are sometimes manufactured without regard to warp, and aluminum arrows can become bent through use or from striking other arrows or hard objects. Arrows can also become bent from being pulled from a target incorrectly (always pull straight out).

Carbon and composite arrows are prone to splintering, although not nearly as much as wood or fiberglass arrows are. To check for splits in an arrow, visually inspect it while holding it by the nock and point ends. Look especially at the areas right around the point and nock. Do not run your hand along it, especially on a fiberglass or carbon shaft; this can cause very painful splinters. Another method of checking an arrow is to hold it by the point and tap it against your opposite palm. A good arrow will ring hollow, and a splintered arrow will rattle. Also, you can flex the arrow *very lightly*—the splinters will stand out. Any splintered arrow should be discarded. They are unsafe to shoot and could injure your hand when you pull them from a target.

More to choose and use

REPAIRING ARROW RESTS

Arrow rests come in many styles, the simplest being the shelf of the bow. When shooting off the shelf, the edge of the shelf eventually wears down, creating a crown that the arrow can no longer rest on. Repairs include carefully filing a new shelf in place or squaring off the crown. If too much of the shelf has been damaged, a quick-fix arrow rest can be fashioned using a bent paper clip stuck upright into the rubber grip of the handle.

Stick-on arrow rests may become worn as well, and they should be replaced when they no longer hold the arrow in position. Clean the area of the bow handle with rubbing alcohol, and attach a new arrow rest in position. Some adjustable rests come with replacement parts, which are available through your archery retailer and sometimes directly from the manufacturer.

Once an arrow rest has been repaired or replaced, the nock locator must be realigned on the bowstring. Rest a bow square on the new arrow rest and measure the nock locator height on the string as you did when you first set up your equipment. With any luck, the new arrow rest will be in the same location as the old one, but be prepared to adjust the nock locator height on the bowstring just in case. If you outline the old arrow rest with a pencil or Sharpie before removing it, you can use the outline as a guide to get a little closer to the position of the old rest when installing the new one.

REPAIRING ARROWS

Usually not much can be done to repair arrows that are split or cracked. Even if the cracks are sealed, the arrow would be unbalanced compared with the rest of the arrows, and it wouldn't fly straight.

Wood and aluminum arrows that have become crooked can be straightened with some effort. First, keep in mind that wood is a natural material and is prone to warping. It's best to try to prevent the warps in the first place by keeping the arrows in a dry storage place and out of wet or humid conditions. Also, store wood arrows flat and not leaning against boxes or walls where they can take on a warp. If they are already warped, you can try steaming the shaft and bending it gently with your hands until straight.

Aluminum arrows can also be straightened using a special tool called an arrow straightener. This tool measures the degree of bend and also bends the arrow back into shape using an adjustable bending arm. Tools like this are often found at archery retail shops. If the bend is minor, you can usually straighten the arrow somewhat by hand.

Regardless of the color or style of your fletching, or whether it is made of feathers or plastic vanes, it can work its way loose or become cut or torn. When buying new arrows, a quick step that can help keep the fletching in place is to spot the end of each fletching with a drop of fletching glue. The bead of glue will protect the edges from lifting off the arrow shaft should the arrow go all the way through a target. Fletching sometimes becomes cut or torn when arrows hit each other on the target face. Minor cuts or flaws usually don't affect arrow flight much, and you can continue to use the arrow as is.

If a fletching edge has come loose, a little fletching glue will seal the fletching back onto the shaft. If the fletching has come all the way off, you should replace that feather or vane for optimum arrow flight. Fletching jigs work slightly differently according to the make and model, but generally they have a sloped rest for the arrow and a rotating base that aligns the position of each vane. Be sure to use a jig that has the same right, left, or straight degree of helical slope as the remaining fletching on the arrow.

First, remove any residual fletching glue from the arrow and clean the area with rubbing alcohol. Place the arrow in the jig, positioning the rotating base with the proper position for the vane. Clamp the vane (without glue) onto the jig and verify the position. Note whether the base of the vane is flush against the arrow shaft, and make any corrections on the jig adjustments as necessary. When you are satisfied with the fit, remove the clamp with the vane in it and spread a thin bead of fletching glue along the base of the fletching. It's important to use just a thin bead of glue; excess glue can result in poor drying and eventually sloppy arrow flight. Replace the clamp in the jig and press the fletching into place on the arrow shaft. Allow the fletching to dry before removing the arrow from the jig. The drying time will vary based on the type of glue used. Inspect the vane for proper adhesion. Place a small drop of glue on all the ends of every vane, and allow that glue to dry before shooting.

Traveling With Your Equipment

When traveling with your equipment, carry it in a well-protected case. Many hard-side cases are available that are suitable to check as airline baggage. Travel restrictions may prohibit you from carrying equipment on board many forms of public transportation without checking it. Always call ahead and speak to the transportation center to be sure.

Cases are available to hold your bow, arrows, accessories, and spare parts. Soft-side cases, such as backpack cases, are great in cars or on the range (figure 10.3). Whenever you travel, always take spare parts and tools with you—don't depend on the kindness of strangers to fix your equipment on location. Your archery toolkit should include the following:

- Cyanoacrylate (CA) glue
- Serving thread
- Backup arrow rest
- Backup bowstring (for recurve bow)
- Spare plunger, set the same way as your current plunger
- Backup finger tab
- Backup sling
- Spare nock locators

10.3 Soft- and hard-side equipment cases.

- Nockset pliers
- Masking tape
- Allen wrenches

Bows can be stored safely in their carrying cases or, in the case of inexpensive one-piece bows, by hanging them horizontally on hooks. For a competition-grade takedown bow, you can also rest the unstrung bow in a bow stand created to hold the bow when it is not being shot. Be sure all your equipment is safe from weather conditions as well as rodents and insects. Bows and arrows that are left leaning against walls or other surfaces tend to warp, so be sure to protect your investment by storing everything carefully.

Buying and Selling Used Equipment

Archers often get great deals on used equipment if they are careful shoppers and are willing to walk away from a bad deal. Always be sure the equipment is sized to your abilities and needs. There's no sense in buying a used bow that's priced right but is too heavy or light for you. It's equally inadvisable to buy used arrows that don't match your bow or even each other. In other words, if you're buying used equipment, know exactly what you're looking for before you start.

Inspect the equipment to be sure it is in good repair before you make the purchase. Make sure all the parts are there—it may be impossible to get replacement parts for older equipment. Check for signs of wear or damage, and be sure all serial numbers and bow measurements are still visible on the labels; serial numbers will give you important information regarding the bow's specs and any relevant warranty guidelines. If possible, try out the equipment prior to making the purchase. Be prepared to replace all strings and cables once you've purchased the equipment. You don't know how long it's been since the last replacement, and it's best to get a clean start with new ones.

Used equipment is sold in a multitude of ways, including at online auctions and on message boards. When selling used equipment, be fair with the buyer. If your equipment has a defect or has sustained enough wear or damage to raise safety concerns, you shouldn't be selling it. Cosmetic issues are typically acceptable, but selling unsafe equipment is never okay. Don't sell faulty equipment if it means someone might get hurt. Make sure the buyer gets all the pieces and parts required for the equipment to work properly along with any printed instructions or documentation.

GENERAL MAINTENANCE

The term *tiller* is used to describe a bow measurement that helps ensure that the top and bottom limbs are drawing back at the same rate. Tiller is determined by the distance between the base of the top or bottom limb and the bowstring, and it is measured using the ruler on the side of your bow square (figure 10.4). The distance should be slightly lower on the bottom limb by about 1/4 inch (0.6 cm). On some competition bows the top measurement is different from the bottom; on others it is equal. Many bow manufacturers specify optimum tiller adjustment in the paperwork that comes with their bows. However you determine tiller, be sure to write the measurements down.

Tiller is changed by adjusting one limb bolt slowly until the bottom limb tiller is 1/4 inch (0.6 cm) lower than the top limb tiller. Remember that adjusting the limb bolt to change tiller also affects draw weight; turning the limb bolt clockwise increases weight, whereas turning it counterclockwise decreases weight. Therefore, it's important to know which way you're adjusting the limb bolts to achieve the appropriate tiller and draw weight for your bow.

Check the tiller measurement from time to time to see whether the limbs are flexing at different rates. If the tiller measurements differ more than 1/4 inch (0.6 cm) on a regular basis despite making adjustments, the limbs may be behaving differently and may need to be replaced. When in doubt, check with your local archery retailer or consult the bow manufacturer's paperwork that came with your bow.

10.4 **Measuring tiller.**

Brace height is the distance between the bowstring and the pivot point on the bow handle. Using a bowstring of the proper measurement for your bow, you can measure this distance using a bow square and note it for future reference. The ideal brace height is determined, in part, by the overall length of your bow. Most bow manufacturers provide the desired brace height in the bow's documentation. If you're unsure of the correct brace height for your bow length, check with your instructor or coach. Brace height is important because it affects the performance of the bow; brace height that is too high or too low can reduce accuracy, and brace height that is inconsistent can impair bow performance and tune.

Double-check the brace height periodically. It may change as a result of string stretch. If so, you can twist the bowstring before installing it on the bow to shorten the string and raise the brace height back to its proper distance. If you install a new string and notice that the brace height is incorrect, this means that the string was not made to the proper length or that it needs to be twisted prior to being installed.

The alignment of the bowstring with the centers of both limbs, in relation to the center shot of the bow, should be checked periodically as well. Several low-cost tools on the market can help you observe this alignment easily by making it simple to accurately line up the bowstring along the limbs and with the arrow (figure 10.5). Misalignment can be caused by a number of factors, including twisted bow limbs. Limbs may become twisted as a result of improper storage (including being left in a hot car for a prolonged period) or improper stringing.

If you suspect limb twist, bring the bow back to your archery retailer to see if repair is possible. Limb twist is typically not covered under warranty, so take good care of your limbs to avoid twisting.

Once your limbs have been slowly adjusted up to their maximum weight (remember, slow increases over a long period of time), it may be time to upgrade to heavier limbs. Keep in mind that you will need time

10.5 **Checking limb alignment.**

to adjust to the new draw weight, so increase the weight gradually to avoid injury. Generally speaking, when shifting from a lighter weight such as a 16-pound (7.3 kg) bow, you may be able to advance directly into a 20-pound (9 kg) bow. However, at weights above 20 pounds, increasing in increments of no more than 2 pounds (approximately 1 kg) is strongly recommended. A compound bow is designed to adjust the draw weight easily. Use a hex wrench on the top and bottom limb bolts. The bow's instructions should tell you how many turns are required to change the weight by 1 pound (about 0.5 kg). Be sure to adjust both limbs equally, or tiller will be off.

On Target

Keeping your equipment happy and healthy involves a periodic inspection of measurements and potential wear. Keep a notebook with the measurements recorded for reference, and always inspect your equipment for safety prior to using it. Proper storage of equipment helps lengthen its usable life span. Store bows in their travel cases or on bow stands to limit stress on the limbs.

Competition

Participation in archery clubs and competitions can help you have fun with the sport and actually make you a better archer. Preparing for competitions helps focus your practice time and supports your improvement through the process of setting goals and measuring results. Participating in a club program, such as USA Archery's Junior Olympic Archery Development (JOAD) or Adult Archery program, connects you with other archers of various skill levels and with archery coaches who can help you improve your shooting and competition performance.

Target archery has so many games and categories that it would be impossible to list them all. Generally, competitive categories are set according to age, gender, ability, and type of equipment. Competition formats also vary according to the types of targets shot at, the distance of the targets, and the number of targets or arrows shot during the competition. The event format is generally determined by the national or international organization that sanctions the event.

Types of Archery Competitions

Local archery clubs may be affiliated with one or more of the national or international organizations. As a result, you might find several types of archery competitions at these clubs, or you may find certain types but not others. In general terms, enough crossover occurs among archers that you should at least be knowledgeable about other forms of competitions. The resources section at the back of this book includes contact information for a number of organizations that regularly hold various types of competitions. Three common forms of archery competitions are target archery, field archery, and 3D archery.

Target Archery

Target archery is found in both world-class tournaments and more informal settings, such as club practice rounds, leagues, and local competitions. It involves standing at a shooting line with other archers and shooting at a round target face at a known distance (figure 11.1).

Target archery is usually shot in a series of ends of three or six arrows, and competitors may shoot a single distance or multiple distances. Whistle commands—often heard during a tournament

11.1 Target archery.

as loud beeps—signal archers to approach the shooting line, shoot their arrows, and retrieve arrows as a group. The archers all know how many total points are possible in that tournament, as well as the size of the target face, which may vary according to the tournament rules. Many tournaments call for a double line, which means that archers take turns shooting in groups, and then all archers pull arrows together. At all tournaments, archers are required to score in groups, so three or four archers often share a target and take turns shooting at it. When the group scores their arrows, one person generally "calls," or states arrow values, while two other people serve as scorekeepers, each with a separate set of cards. A fourth person may assist with electronic scoring, if that's used at the tournament, or otherwise help to mark arrow holes. Generally, competing archers pull their own arrows from the target.

USA Archery is the national governing body for the Olympic sport of archery in the United States. USA Archery selects and trains Olympic, Paralympic, World Championship, and World Cup teams and also works to develop archery at the grassroots level across the United States.

USA Archery hosts key national tournaments every year, including indoor and outdoor National Championship events for adults and youth, as well as the USAT Qualifier Series, a series of events at which youth and adult archers compete for spots on the National Team for archery. The organization also educates and certifies archery instructors and coaches, and sanctions hundreds of regional, state, and local events each year.

The U.S. Olympic and Paralympic teams are selected via team trials, as are teams for World Cups and World Championship events. Other events may be subject to team trials as well. Only three men and three women are selected every four years to represent the United States at the Olympic Games; participation in the Paralympic Games depends on the number of athletes qualified for the divisions being offered.

USA Archery provides tournament opportunities for all archers. It offers beginners many ways to engage with the sport of archery, including nationwide programs that teach archery and allow participants to progress in the sport through ongoing classes and instruction.

Field Archery

Field archery, a spin-off of target archery, began during the 1930s to fill the needs of many archers to compete in less formalized settings (figure 11.2). Field archery was also originally developed to hone skills for bowhunting. Since its inception, field archery has become extremely popular, and many archers enjoy practicing their skills at field and target archery alike, as well as 3D.

A field archery range looks a little like a golf course, with a roving path through a natural setting. The archers shoot from marked stakes—basically, stakes or ground markers that designate the distance from the target. The archers rove through the course in small groups taking turns shooting at the same targets and recording their own scores as they move to the next target. The distances are measured in yards. The targets in the range are set up at various known distances of 18 to 80 yards; some require archers to shoot from several stakes of varying degrees of difficulty.

Because field archery is a roving course and archers travel in small groups, there is no central whistle command. The groups move at their own pace, and the target layout ensures that no archer is ever shooting toward another shooting station anywhere on the course. The typical field range course has 14 targets on it, and many ranges have more than one course on the property. The typical number of archers per group is four.

Field archery uses paper target faces, and paper animal target faces are used in some tournaments. Because these tournaments are shot in natural settings, there are generally no dress codes. Although recurve bows can be used, many archers prefer compound bows; many traditional and barebow archers also enjoy field archery. Rear sights, mechanical string releases, and magnifying sight aids are allowed in most divisions, but allowable accessories depend on the type of bow.

The National Field Archery Association (NFAA) is the organizer of field archery clubs and tournaments in the United States. Headquartered in Yankton, South Dakota, it offers tournament divisions ranging from barebow (generally a simple recurve or compound bow with no sights or other advantages) to freestyle, in which almost anything goes in terms of technology. The NFAA hosts local, regional,

11.2 **Field archery.**

state, and national competitions both indoors and outdoors. An international competition is also hosted through NFAA's affiliated organization, the International Field Archery Association (IFAA).

Internationally, World Archery sponsors the World Archery Field Championships, which is a biannual event. In this format, field archers shoot at targets at marked distances on one day and unmarked distances the next; elimination rounds, in which archers shoot in head-to-head matches, are also shot to determine medal winners. USA Archery mimics this format at its own U.S. National Field Championships, which is the organization's only major field archery tournament.

3D Archery

The sport of 3D archery has developed relatively recently. It involves a roving course in a format similar to that of field archery, except that the targets are life-size, three-dimensional foam animals set up in natural settings at known and unknown distances alongside the trails (figure 11.3). Each 3D target has scoring circles molded into its side located approximately where the kill zone would be on a live animal.

Archers travel the course in small groups taking turns shooting at the targets. Because this is a game of unknown and known distances, and you have already learned how quickly an arrow can drop in flight, you can see that 3D archery is as much about judging distances as it is about being an accurate shot. Archers compensate by using fast compound bows with flatter arrow trajectories and often

11.3 **3D archery.**

some form of magnifying front sight; however, there is no substitute for the skill of judging distance. Archers are not allowed to use distance-measuring devices; nor are they allowed to mark their bows to aid in measuring distances.

A 3D course is set up in secret just prior to the tournament, so the archers usually don't get a first look at the course prior to shooting at each station. This lack of prior knowledge makes the course extremely challenging. This type of competition is widely popular because of its simulated hunting environment and because of the vast array of technology permissible. Often, tournaments have entry fees that are divided among the division winners.

Two popular national organizations that offer and coordinate separate 3D tournaments are the Archery Shooters Association (ASA), located near Atlanta, Georgia, and the International Bowhunting Organization (IBO) in Vermillion, Ohio. Both organizations have affiliated clubs in many parts of the United States. ASA is primarily a tournament organization; it hosts qualifying tournaments as well as a national circuit that has become immensely popular. IBO clubs host local and regional tournaments, and the national organization hosts annual championships that are very popular. The IBO also has bowhunter education programs in addition to their tournaments.

━━━━━ *More to choose and use* ━━━━━

BENEFITS OF WORKING WITH A COACH

Let's assume for the moment that you've contacted a nearby club and narrowed down the style of archery you want to pursue. You've taken a big step away from being a casual recreational archer toward becoming a competition archer. To compete for points with any sort of consistency, you should consider using the services of a certified instructor or coach (figure 11.4). A certified archery instructor or coach is a trained person who observes your shooting technique, listens to your goals, and makes specific recommendations for improvement. A coach acts as a partner in your growth as a competitor, and can provide occasional instruction or a more intensive level of coaching, depending on your needs. USA Archery and the National Field Archery Association currently share a certification program that ensures that instructors and coaches are trained to specific standards and, depending on their level of certification, undergo a background check and SafeSport training. SafeSport is a program to

help sport instructors "recognize, reduce, and respond to misconduct in sport" (http://safesport.org/what-is-safesport).

The key to becoming a proficient archer is to develop a consistent form. If you attend an archery tournament, even a national championship, you'll see many forms and techniques—even among the top archers. Even so, what you'll also notice among the elite is their ability to duplicate that same form or technique shot after shot.

An archery coach sees you from the outside. While shooting a bow, your own perception of what you are or aren't doing is extremely limited. A coach who has been trained to observe and provide positive feedback based on that observation can greatly assist in identifying and correcting inconsistent form.

Although your shooting technique may feel right to you, you aren't in the best position to see what's actually going on. However, a certified instructor or coach is. Your coach can observe shot after shot and see whether each part of your body, each motion and reaction, is the same as the one before. Through carefully worded instructions, a good coach will increase your overall consistency and your resulting tournament scores.

A coach can start out as a total stranger you hire for an hour to show you how to hold the bow upright. But remember, you're choosing someone you want on your side, and you need to feel comfortable around that person. Almost all archery clubs are run by a certified instructor or coach, and this is a major advantage of choosing a club that's affiliated with a national organization; you're likely to have some great coaching resources close at hand. It's common for coaches to charge for lessons, whether group or individual, and rates vary from coach to coach.

Key factors to consider when choosing a coach are personality (do you respond well to the coach's manner of speaking and teaching?), time (do you each have the time to work together?), space (where will you meet for lessons?), and of course, budget. When you meet with your coach, be sure to discuss exactly what you hope to accomplish and the kinds of tournaments you wish to compete in. This way, you'll both have a measuring stick in place to judge your progress and clearly evaluate the effectiveness of your relationship. In general, you should feel comfortable with your coach, motivated by your sessions together, and supported in reaching your goals as an athlete. If you find that you aren't making progress toward your goals, do not understand the directives your coach gives you, or aren't having fun, you may need to communicate your concerns more directly to your coach or consider finding a coach who is a better match for you.

Take it to the range

Preparing for a Competition

So now you're set to compete—you've developed a practice schedule, you have a positive relationship with a coach who has helped make your shooting form and your scores consistent, and you've chosen an archery competition. It's time to make your pretournament checklist.

Learn the Rules and Regulations   First of all, learn the rules of the particular tournament you are attending, and be sure you understand them. Mostly, you'll need to know what style or size of targets are to be used, the distances to be shot, the number of arrows you'll be allowed, any time limits for shooting, and the equipment that's legal. You can usually find the rules of the tournament by contacting the tournament director listed on the tournament announcement. Tournaments are often guided by the standard rules of the national organizations that sanction them. Investigate where and when the tournament will take place, and whether it's a day trip or would require an overnight stay. It's best to start with a local event to keep costs down and so you are familiar with the surroundings and people for your first competition.

Check Your Equipment Now that you know the rules, make sure your equipment is legal and that there is a division within the event for the equipment you have. Now's not the time to radically change your equipment to fit the event—just make sure it's legal and in good repair. Make a list of your equipment, and make sure that you pack everything you intend to take, including a spotting scope, stool, umbrella, or even a pop-up tent. Some, but not all, tournaments offer concessions, so bring the drinks and snacks you want. Bringing your own food makes it easy to avoid caffeine and excess sugar and to stick with water, sport drinks, and healthier snacks such as fruit, nuts, and nutritious sandwiches, as needed.

Inspect all your equipment, and make any needed repairs on your bow or arrows. Once repairs have been made, continue to practice with the repaired equipment to ensure that no changes have occurred and that everything still feels natural and comfortable. You should have complete confidence in your equipment.

Even with confidence in your equipment, accidents and breakages happen at the worst possible moments. And, generally, once the event has started, officials won't stop the clock to allow you to make extensive repairs. *Always* bring along backup accessories (figure 11.5). You should have additional arrows that perform the same as your main tournament arrows and an extra bowstring that has been used in practice and performs the same as your main bowstring. Other important backups include a broken-in finger tab, a spare sling, an extra arrow rest, a backup mechanical release aid if you use a compound bow, and an extra plunger if you use a recurve.

In addition, bring along your bow square and nockset pliers to measure all your critical dimensions prior to the tournament to ensure that nothing has shifted during travel. Have a toolkit handy that fits all the screws and bolts on your bow and accessories. Some participants duplicate their entire archery rigs, including the bow. Archery shouldn't stretch your budget, though, so don't go overboard in the replacements. But do have on hand any replacement items you think you might need.

Simulate the Event Once you've learned the rules and selected your equipment, it's time to modify your practice to simulate the tournament as much as possible. This means switching over to official target faces if possible, remeasuring your target distances so they are the same as those of the upcoming event, practicing during the same time of day, and even getting in some practice on the very range the event will be on if it's a permanent archery range to which you can gain access. If the range location is not set up but

11.5 Bring duplicates of essential equipment (such as a bow) to the competition.

is in close geographic proximity, you might visit it to walk around and get a feel for it. This way, you won't be distracted on the day of the tournament with new sights or sounds. Talk to archers who have competed at that event before. Ask how many archers generally compete, their ages, where to park, and other questions. When you walk into the event, you want to feel as though you've already been there a thousand times. Your pretournament practice should include shooting the same number of arrows within the same time frame allowed, and even scoring your practice shots on the official scorecards if they are available. Shooting around other people (e.g., by attending a league or just practicing at your local archery range instead of at home) can also be great practice for your tournament. The purpose of simulating the event as best you can is to lessen the emotional effect of actually competing.

Determine your tournament goals and motivations prior to the tournament, just as if it were another practice session. Your goal for your first competition is to learn how to shoot in a tournament. The purposes of competing as a beginner are to gain experience and learn to shoot your form consistently under pressure—basically, to have fun and gain confidence. Nothing else matters or should be expected.

Develop Your Mental Game *Mental game* is a term that covers whatever you do to stay calm and focused on your technique regardless of your performance and despite any distractions that may take place in the shooting environment. The best archery advice (arguably) ever given is as follows: The only arrow that matters is the one on the string. You can't get shot arrows back, and you can't do anything about the arrows you have yet to shoot. Shoot with a short memory, and concentrate on every arrow as if it's the only shot that day. Develop your mental game during practice, and follow the routines exactly.

One of the most important aspects of a good mental game is consistency. Whether you employ visualization, positive affirmations, a repeatable set of steps, or all three, you want to use them consistently for each shot you take. Visualization (imagining yourself completing the action the way you want to) is a powerful tool to help you start the shot in a positive way. Affirmation (telling yourself what you will achieve on the shot) should be specific and positive. Using a set of steps that you repeat to execute each shot is a critical piece of the shooting process, and will especially help if you're ever under pressure in a competition. That set of steps becomes a routine that will be the same in your backyard or local archery range as it is in local or national championships.

Remember, your brain always responds to and learns better from positive, constructive criticism than from negative feedback. In other words, telling yourself what you're going to do right on a shot is much more effective than telling yourself what not to do wrong. Reinforce the good and move on, shooting one arrow at a time.

Give it a go

ATTENDING A COMPETITION

The number one rule about arriving at a competition is to arrive early so you don't have to rush. Sign in with the tournament director, find out your lane assignment (where you will be shooting), and review any rules you might have questions about. This includes who to turn to if there is a scoring dispute (an event judge) and where to take your scores when you are finished shooting. At many tournaments, you have to have your equipment inspected by the event judge to ensure that it's legal for that event. Check your name and division in the shooting roster so that you can be in position to shoot at the time indicated, and review your target assignment and shooting order (A, B, C, D). Take your time putting your bow together to be sure you're doing it correctly. Say hi to your target mates, and then find a place to put your jacket and other gear. Once that's done, and your equipment has been inspected, take a few minutes to stretch out and get your muscles warmed up. At your first event, pay attention so that you fully absorb what is going on around you. Once you have become experienced with tournaments, consider bringing music, a book, or some other item that will help you stay relaxed between ends.

As with any sport, informal etiquette is nearly as important as the formal event rules. Many events are run by volunteers who have devoted a considerable amount of time and effort to help participating archers have a good time. You may be asked to help move targets, help score, or perform any number of small tasks. Be prepared to help out as needed—it makes the event run more smoothly and helps you become part of the archery community more quickly. Another point of etiquette is to remain quiet while on the shooting line, and to be respectful of others' personal and competitive space. You will have a lane designated to you—a set area in which to shoot. When in your lane, hold your bow upright as opposed to sideways, so that it isn't in anyone else's space, and be sure your body, bow, and scope are in your own lane. Also, if the archer next to you is at full draw and you finish first, it is considered polite to remain on the line until the archer is no longer at full draw.

A tournament may be the first time your performance is compared with that of other archers. Although it's tempting to focus on this comparison, it's vital that in your own mind you are competing only with yourself. At first, your only goal should be to gain experience and confidence. As you become a better archer, you may also set a score-based goal for the event, but you should never think about your score while you are competing, only after you're done. Be polite and welcoming to your fellow competitors, and try never to compare your scores to theirs. Many events have a running scoreboard, or leader board, on display. Try not to focus on it; keep your mind on your technique and your mental game instead. Many other archers will be doing the same, so in general, scores and results are not a great topic of conversation at tournaments.

If you attend a tournament with your coach, odds are that the coach will not be able to speak to you during the actual shooting. You'll be on your own for that. Coaches in large tournaments, however, are often seen behind the waiting line observing their archers. Following each scoring end, you might be permitted to speak with your coach if you walk to where he or she is. Keep in mind that the coach's job during the tournament is to reinforce your mental game and your shot execution—it is *not* to change your style or your goals. Your coach is there to encourage and support you, while helping you to ask the best of yourself. Resist the temptation to ask what you are doing wrong, but instead focus on what you're doing right, and repeat with your coach the same positive reinforcement routine that you used during practice.

On Target

Competing in archery tournaments is fun and exciting, and archers make lifelong friends when they join clubs, leagues, and tournaments. Archery tournaments may give you the opportunity to advance in national standings and perhaps even to represent your country in international competitions. A tournament, no matter how small or big, should be used as a learning exercise—namely, to gain experience and to practice your physical and mental techniques under pressure. Your goals for the event should be thought out well in advance and adhered to during the event, and having fun should be goal number one, whether you're competing at the Olympic or Paralympic Games or at the local archery range.

12

Traditional Archery

Archery's roots are steeped in tradition, and it's truly an ancient sport, with roots that date back over 5,000 years. Bows and arrows have been used to address such basic human needs as safety and survival, and for thousands of years, they have been used to hunt wild game, which is today referred to as bowhunting.

The sport has recently evolved quite dramatically, undergoing more technical evolution in the last 60 years than it did in the previous 5,000. Compound bows, which were invented in the mid-1960s, took the archery world by storm, as did the modern recurve bow, particularly with the gradual additions of sights, stabilizers, and other accessories that are the norm today.

Although the vast majority of today's archers use Olympic-style recurve bows or compound bows, some archers prefer to stay close to the sport's roots by participating in what is known as traditional archery. This designation refers to the use of traditional archery equipment that is essentially stripped down to the basic components of bow, bowstring, and arrow. Some archery organizations, and even individual clubs, promote this style of archery, which may include the use of longbows, traditional recurve bows, homemade self bows (i.e., bows made from a single piece of wood), and traditional bows from other countries (e.g., the Mongolian horse bow). Traditional archery often includes the use of wood arrows and various leather accessories, and typically prohibits the use of sights and arrow rests (archers shoot off the bow's shelf).

Traditional archery, whether enjoyed on a regular target range or on a roving field archery range, is seeing an increase in popularity thanks to the depictions of traditional archery in movies such as *The Hunger Games*. Have you seen the character of Katniss Everdeen running through the woods hunting squirrels while wearing a back quiver and shooting her hand-fletched arrows from her longbow? This is a perfect example of traditional archery, as used in bowhunting.

Many of today's tournaments offer categories for traditional archers. However, there are specific rules for competition in traditional and barebow divisions, which generally prohibit the use of sights, stabilizers, clickers, and in some cases, arrow rests. Some methods of aiming are also restricted. Because the rules for competing with traditional or barebow equipment vary considerably, check with the organization hosting your tournament to learn the types of equipment that are permitted in each division.

Why traditional archery? One of the great benefits of this style of shooting is that it strips away all distractions—it's just you and the bow and the arrow. Removing the technology from the equation allows you to focus just on form, and it can feel freeing and fun to shoot at a target with little expectation of hitting the middle. True, the very best traditional archers accomplish great feats using traditional equipment (Howard Hill, known as the world's greatest archer, was champion at *196* field archery competitions), but in truth, most people shoot traditional archery for the love of the bow and arrow, without a high expectation of score.

You can do it

Traditional Bows

The craftsmanship of many of the wood bows is breathtaking. A high-quality handmade bow can give you the sensation of holding a fly rod. Bows are made of various types of woods: bamboo, maple, yew, ash, oak, and hickory, to name just a few. The longbow—technically, a self bow—has a different feel than that of a traditional recurve bow, and the many other variations on the traditional bow have their own distinctive characteristics. The wonderful thing about traditional bows is that they often also speak to a culture's history; the Mongolian horse bow, for example, is used today in ceremonial archery festivals, but it was an important part of Mongolia's military history. The Mongolian horse bow, like the yumi, a Japanese traditional bow, is an example of a primitive bow: a traditional bow recreated as it was shot many hundreds or thousands of years ago.

The longbow gets its name from literally being a longer bow—often extending to the height of its owner. Though regarded sometimes as less accurate than the traditional recurve, the longbow may feel easier to draw because the pull weight is dispersed across a larger surface area. A longbow can be laminated (i.e., multiple layers of wood are glued together to construct the bow's limbs), or it can be a self bow fashioned from a single piece of any number of types of wood. Unlike the distinctive curves on the limbs of a recurve bow, the limbs on a longbow have a flatter curve and straighter appearance. The longbow consists of a handle, which is fairly round, and limbs, which are fairly narrow (figure 12.1).

The feeling of the bow varies depending on how it was built and the type(s) of wood used to make it. Experienced traditional archers say that they can feel a significant difference between a high-end longbow and a longbow marketed toward beginners. The handle of the longbow—specifically, its grip—is sometimes wrapped in leather and has a wooden shelf from which the arrow is shot.

Although it is possible to purchase a takedown recurve with a traditional look and feel, a true traditional recurve is a one-piece bow. The traditional recurve bow has two defining characteristics: (1) an obvious curve to its limb that "recurves" toward the archer and (2) its length, which is generally much shorter than that of the longbow (figure 12.2). Being a shorter bow, it can tend to have a stouter pull than that of the longbow, but the trade-off is in accuracy: A traditional recurve is generally more accurate than a longbow.

12.1 Traditional longbow.

Like the longbow, the traditional recurve bow can be made of a variety of woods, and may have a fiberglass overlay. Higher-end recurve bows may be made of more exotic woods; the type of wood not only changes the feel of the shot, but also packs a powerful visual impact. Many people who enjoy traditional archery appreciate the craftsmanship that goes into building a longbow or a one-piece recurve, the various colors incorporated into the bow, and the unique feel of each bow based on the particular way it was built.

12.2   **Traditional recurve bow.**

More to choose and use

ACCESSORIES

Depending on your preferences and the rules of any competitions you're interested in, an arrow rest, typically a flat piece of leather, and an arrow plate, which mounts on the sight window to the side of the shelf, may be installed. Both of these items provides a consistent and smooth surface over which the arrow travels as it leaves the bowstring, preventing wear on the bow.

Some traditional recurves and longbows come with bowstrings; others need bowstrings made for them. Remember that, just as with a modern Olympic recurve or compound bow, the string you purchase must be made according to the length and style of your bow. Many traditional archers prefer the look and feel of a Flemish twist string, which has a special type of end loop to fit more easily over the limb notch of a traditional recurve bow or longbow (figure 12.3). Any bowstring will have a nock locator installed or tied onto the string;

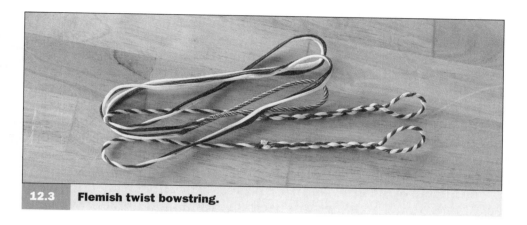

12.3 Flemish twist bowstring.

for expert help on setting the nock height and tuning the bow, work with the retailer from whom you purchase the bow.

What other accessories does the traditional archer require besides a bow, bowstring, and arrow plate? Arrows. Traditional archers often favor wood arrows made of cedar, which are often stained various colors for aesthetic purposes. Many traditional archers make their own wooden arrows, although they can be purchased premade from traditional archery specialists. Like a modern arrow, a wooden arrow must have a shaft that is tapered at both ends, a point that goes over one end of the shaft, a nock that goes over the opposite end of the shaft to fasten it onto the bowstring, and fletchings to steer the arrow in flight. Additionally, many traditional archers crest their arrows using paint, often creating beautiful designs. Fletchings are almost always feathers as opposed to vanes; they clear the bow more easily as the arrow is released, are more forgiving in flight, and of course are more authentic as part of the traditional archery experience. The length and type of the feather depends on the archer's preference and on the intended use. Many traditional archers favor 5-inch (12.7 cm) feathers, which create extra drag but improve arrow stability (figure 12.4).

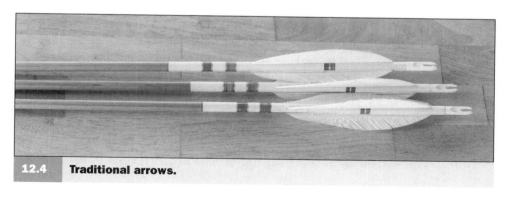

12.4 Traditional arrows.

Traditional archers need very basic equipment: an arrow plate, a bowstring, and arrows. So what do they use for personal accessories? All archers are strongly encouraged to use an arm guard, and traditional archers are no exception. Most traditional bows are made in heavier draw weights and are designed to be drawn back and shot relatively quickly. As a result of pulling this heavier weight, there is a greater likelihood of a painful bruise if there is a form error or just not enough string clearance when the arrow is released. Therefore, a traditional arm guard may be used, which often laces along the forearm and is made of leather.

The fingers of the draw hand are protected by either a shooting glove or a finger tab. The finger tab used for traditional archery typically does not have metal plates, ledges, or spacers. For a truly authentic experience, a tab of leather, made of one or more layers, is used. A special three-fingered shooting glove that has leather just to protect the first three fingers may also be used. There's little major difference between the degree of traditional archery success achieved with a glove versus a tab; the choice is a matter of personal preference. What matters is that the finger protection selected is effective at guarding the fingertips, and that the leather provides a smooth surface that the string can slide off upon release.

Traditional archers also use a quiver to hold their arrows, although unlike compound and modern recurve archers, true traditionalists use a back quiver. Back quivers are made of leather or other durable, historically authentic materials, stitched together to form a long, tubelike holder for the arrows. The back quiver is mounted on the back and attached with a strap that extends from one shoulder to the opposite side of the body, securing under the arm and across the chest. The nocks of the arrows are positioned behind the draw-side shoulder; a right-handed archer reaches over the right shoulder to pull an arrow from the quiver, and vice versa.

Take it to the range

Shooting Technique

Once you are outfitted, it's time to begin shooting. The form used for modern recurve and compound bow shooting differs somewhat from that used with a traditional recurve or longbow, although the steps are somewhat similar. Many of the principles that apply to shooting recurve laid out in chapter 4 apply here as well. However, traditional archery is a highly personalized area, and many experienced traditional archers approach technique somewhat differently. A certified coach or instructor who has experience with traditional archery can help you perfect your form. Practice and experiment to determine what works best for you.

1. Stance. Stand with one foot on either side of the shooting line, with a bit more weight on your front foot than on your rear foot. Your feet should be about shoulder-width apart (figure 12.5). Some traditional archers favor a square stance, perpendicular to the target, over the slightly open stance (the toe of the bow-side foot aligned with the ball of the draw-side foot) recommended for recurve archers.

2. Nocking the arrow. Take an arrow from your back quiver and snap it onto the bowstring (figure 12.6), making sure the nock of the arrow is free of cracks or splinters prior to nocking. Be sure to position the arrow with the index feather facing away from the bow.

12.5 Stance.

12.6 Nocking the arrow.

3. *Hooking the string.* Place your fingers on the bowstring, using the tab or glove. Although finger placement on the string is an individualized decision, using the archer's groove (i.e., placing the string just before the first joint on the index finger, just behind the joint on the middle finger, and just in front of the joint on the third finger) is a perfectly acceptable hook. Keep the back of your hand flat and relaxed, and your wrist straight or with a very slight outward bend (figure 12.7).

12.7 Hooking the string.

4. *Gripping the bow.* Next, place your bow hand on the grip of the bow. If you're using a traditional recurve bow, use a grip position similar to that used with a modern recurve. Find the pressure point on your hand, which is the meaty part at the base of the thumb, next to the lifeline. Then, with your thumb pointed toward the target, gently rest your index finger on the front of the grip, and curl the remaining fingers under with your knuckles pulled back to form a 45-degree angle to the shelf of the bow. If you're shooting a longbow, you can use the traditional recurve grip or try a slightly different grip used by many longbow archers; after finding the correct pressure point on your hand, gently curl your fingers around the grip of the bow (figure 12.8). Keep the thumb and pinkie finger tucked under and close to the palm of your hand. *Note:* Some archers will prefer a split finger hook, while others will be more comfortable shooting with three fingers under the nock of the arrow. This is an individual decision and experimentation is encouraged.

12.8 Gripping the longbow.

5. *Posture.* Check to be sure you have assumed the correct posture for shooting a traditional bow: shoulders straight, low, and relaxed; back flat; and head directed straight toward the target.

Many archers cant the bow (i.e., tilt it to one side) to improve their accuracy. To execute this technique, lean slightly forward as you draw the bow, keeping the head and neck in a natural position, and remain in that posture throughout the shot (figure 12.9).

6. *Drawing.* As with drawing a recurve bow, it's important to use the larger, stronger muscles of your back, not your arm muscles. Bring the back of your draw-side arm and your draw-side scapula back and around your draw-side shoulder as you draw the bow (figure 12.10).

12.9 Canting the bow for traditional archery.

12.10 Drawing the bow.

7. *Anchoring.* Draw to an anchor point on your face, bringing your index finger to the corner of your mouth. Many traditional archers experiment with different anchor points. It is important to make sure your anchor point is consistent (figure 12.11).

12.11 Anchoring.

8. *Transferring.* As you reach your anchor point, continue to hold tension in your draw-side scapula and the back of your draw arm (figure 12.12); this keeps the shot strong and sets up a great release and follow-through. This is a quick and small movement; longbows generally have heavier draw weight and lend themselves to a faster shot sequence than with modern recurve.

12.12 Transferring.

9. *Aiming.* Continue the movement and maintain tension in your back as you aim briefly. If you are shooting instinctively, simply point and shoot at a single area on (or off) the target, without using a reference point.

If you choose to use a reference point, such as the point of the arrow, frame it at the preselected point on the target to aim (figure 12.13).

10. *Releasing and following through.* Let the bowstring roll off your fingertips as you pull your draw hand backward and continue to maintain back tension. Your draw hand should closely follow the line of your face toward the back of your ear, pulled back naturally by the movement of your back muscles (figure 12.14). Keep a relaxed grip on the bow with your grip hand.

12.13 Using a reference point to aim.

12.14 Releasing and following through.

WINDY CONDITIONS

For all archers, weather is an important factor; however, if you choose a traditional bow, Mother Nature can have an even greater impact on your shooting. Because the typical traditional bow setup provides less speed than modern bows, environmental factors such as wind are important to address.

Your stance can have an effect on the way you shoot. Having an open stance helps keep you more stable in the wind. Canting—or tilting—the bow can help you achieve more precise arrow placement in windy conditions.

To learn how this works, head out on a day with a variable breeze and stand about 10 to 15 yards from your target (or at another close, comfortable distance). Start out by waiting for calm, and then shoot three arrows into your target. Now wait for the breeze and shoot an arrow the way you normally would; this will show you the direction in which the wind is carrying your arrows. The wind can change the shape of the arc as well. On the next shot, try canting your bow in the direction you want the arrow to go. Continue practicing this since sometimes the wind can shift while you are shooting.

In other words, if the wind is blowing right to left, try canting to the right. You can experiment with varying degrees of cant, but you should start to see the groups of arrows move toward the right, depending on if the wind is consistent. Remember, too, that learning to read the wind (i.e., knowing the direction it's moving in) is an important skill for any archer.

On Target

Although much research and study has been done on biomechanically proven shooting techniques for modern recurve and compound bows, traditional archery is dedicated to recreating the experience of archers who hunted long ago with simple implements, having learned to shoot from their elders and refined their technique through trial and error. Many archery organizations promote traditional archery and it has gained popularity in recent years. It involves using just the basic items: bow, bowstring, and arrow. Thus, its participants are influenced not only by personal experience with their bows and what feels best to them when shooting, but also by the proven success of skilled longbow and traditional recurve archers who are willing to share their secrets. The steps in this chapter provide a suggested outline for beginners, but as you progress in traditional archery, you should forge your own path along the road toward an authentic archery experience, seeking the help of others along the way.

Resources

Organizations

Archery 360 (News, Information, and Retail Shop Locator)
www.archery360.com

Archery Shooters Association
P.O. Box 399, Kennesaw, GA 30156
770-795-0232
info@asaarchery.com
www.asaarchery.com

International Bowhunting Organization
P.O. Box 398, Vermillion, OH 44089
440-967-2137
www.ibo.net

International Field Archery Association (IFAA)
www.ifaa-archery.org

National Field Archery Association
800 Archery Lane, Yankton, SD 57078
605-260-9279
www.nfaausa.com

SafeSport
1 Olympic Plaza, Colorado Springs, CO 80909
safesport@usoc.org
http://safesport.org

USA Archery
4065 Sinton Road, Suite 110, Colorado Springs, CO 80907
719-866-4576
www.teamusa.org/USA-Archery

World Archery
Avenue de Rhodanie 54 1007, Lausanne, Switzerland
+41 21 6143050
info@archery.org
www.worldarchery.org

Equipment Vendors

3Rivers Archery
Lancaster Archery Supply

Books

Lee, KiSik and Benner, Tyler. 2009. *Total archery: Inside the archer.* Chula Vista, CA: Astra LLC.

USA Archery. 2013. *Archery.* Champaign, IL: Human Kinetics.

About the Writer

Teresa Johnson received USA Archery's 2010 Developmental Coach of the Year Award and has coached recreational and competitive youth and adult archers since 2007. She is a level 4 National Training System (NTS)-certified archery coach and level 3 NTS coach trainer. Johnson has shot compound and recurve bows for over 10 years.

Johnson specializes in public relations. Combining her love of archery with her passion for communications in her daily work, she served as the press attaché for the U.S. archery team at the London 2012 Olympic Games. She also was project coordinator for *Archery* (Human Kinetics, 2013), edited by USA Archery.

Johnson resides in Connecticut with her husband, Butch, a five-time Olympian and Olympic gold medalist in archery.

You'll find other outstanding outdoor sports resources at

www.HumanKinetics.com/outdooractivities

In the U.S. call 1-800-747-4457

Australia 08 8372 0999 • Canada 1-800-465-7301
Europe +44 (0) 113 255 5665 • New Zealand 0800 222 062

HUMAN KINETICS
The Premier Publisher for Sports & Fitness
P.O. Box 5076 • Champaign, IL 61825-5076 USA

eBook
available at
HumanKinetics.com